W9-BPJ-681

A CLASSIC RETELLING

ROMEO
and
Juliet

by William Shakespeare

nextext

Printed in the United States of America.

ISBN 0-618-03146-4

1 2 3 4 5 6 7 — QKT — 06 05 04 03 02 01 00

Picture Acknowledements

Page 11: Alice Buchanan Fort and Herbert S. Kates, Minute History of the Drama. New York: Grosset & Dunlap, Inc., 1935.

Pages 14 & 21: The British Library

Pages 18 & 19: Mansell Collection

Page 20: www.corbis.com/Chris Hellier

Pages 23 & 25: From The Complete Works of Shakespeare edited by David Bevington. Copyright © 1997 by Addison-Wesley Educational Publishers Inc. Reprinted by permission.

Table of Contents

Background 10

The Story of *Romeo and Juliet*

Shakespeare's Theater

Shakespeare's Language

The Characters

The Plot

Shakespeare's Life

A Shakespeare Time Line

ACT ONE
_____

Prologue 28

The Chorus gives a short description of
the story.

Sunday

Scene One 30

In a public place in Verona, Italy, early one
morning, Prince Escalus stops a fight between
the Montagues and Capulets and says that
if any other fights start, he will put the fighters
to death. Romeo is sad because he loves a
woman who doesn't love him.

Scene Two **42**

*When they meet on a street, Paris tells Juliet's
father, Capulet, that he wishes to marry
Juliet. Capulet objects because she is too young
but says he would allow the marriage when
she is older. Capulet invites Paris to a party so
that he can see Juliet. Romeo learns about the
party and decides to go since Rosaline, the
girl he loves, will be there.*

Scene Three **47**

*At the Capulets' house, Lady Capulet and the
Nurse tell Juliet that Paris wishes to marry
her. Juliet agrees to give Paris a chance, even
though she shows little interest in him.*

Scene Four **51**

*Outside the Capulets' house, Romeo and his
friends are on the way to the Capulets' party.
Romeo explains that he is anxious because
of a bad dream. Mercutio teases him by
telling him about the fairy queen Mab, who
gives dreams.*

Scene Five **56**

*Inside the Capulets' house during the party,
Romeo and Juliet meet and fall in love. Tybalt
tries to fight Romeo, but Capulet stops him.*

Scene One **68**
Outside the Capulets' house, Romeo's friends,
Benvolio and Mercutio, try to find him, but he
hides from them.

Scene Two **71**
Outside the Capulets' house, under Juliet's
balcony, Romeo overhears Juliet confess her
love for him. Romeo tells Juliet he loves her.
Juliet sets up a plan for their marriage.

Monday
Scene Three **82**
In Friar Laurence's cell in the monastery, the
friar agrees to marry Romeo and Juliet because
he sees a chance to stop the feud between
the two families.

Scene Four **87**
On a public street, Tybalt challenges Romeo to
fight. Romeo tells the Nurse his plan to marry
Juliet that afternoon. The Nurse will take a rope
ladder to Juliet so Romeo may climb to her
balcony that night.

Scene Five **94**
In the Capulets' orchard, the Nurse tells Juliet
about Romeo's plans for their marriage.

Scene Six **98**

In Friar Laurence's cell, Juliet and Romeo meet
to be married by Friar Laurence.

ACT THREE

Scene One **102**

In a public place, Tybalt, Juliet's cousin, tries to
start a fight with Romeo. Because Romeo has
just married Juliet, he refuses to fight with her
cousin. Mercutio fights with Tybalt. When
Romeo tries to stop the fight, Tybalt uses the
chance to stab Mercutio. Mercutio dies. Romeo
kills Tybalt. Romeo is sent away from the city.

Scene Two **112**

In the Capulets' orchard, the Nurse tells Juliet
that Romeo killed Tybalt. At first Juliet is angry
at Romeo, but then she declares her loyalty
to him. The Nurse promises to bring Romeo to
Juliet that night.

Scene Three **118**

In Friar Laurence's cell, Friar Laurence tells
Romeo that the Prince has sent him away.
Romeo says that death would be better
than being sent away from Juliet. The Nurse
arrives to bring Romeo to Juliet. Friar
Laurence calms Romeo.

Scene Four 125

In a room in the Capulets' house, Capulet
decides that Juliet should marry Paris
on Thursday.

Tuesday

Scene Five 128

Early in the morning, on Juliet's balcony, Romeo
leaves. Romeo has been with Juliet through the
night. Juliet's mother comes to tell her the new
plans for her to marry Paris. When Juliet refuses,
Capulet threatens to throw her out if she
doesn't obey his wishes. The Nurse tells Juliet to
forget Romeo and marry Paris.

ACT FOUR
_____

Scene One 140

In Friar Laurence's cell, Paris is arranging his
wedding when Juliet arrives. Juliet threatens
suicide if Friar Laurence can't stop the
marriage. Friar Laurence suggests a plan to
fake Juliet's death so that Romeo and Juliet
can be together.

Scene Two 145

At the Capulets' house, as part of Friar
Laurence's plan, Juliet tells her father that she

will marry Paris. Capulet decides to move the
marriage to the next day, Wednesday.

Scene Three 148
In Juliet's room, Juliet takes the sleeping drug
that will make her seem to be dead.

Wednesday
Scene Four 150
In the Capulets' house, the Capulets stay up
all night to get ready for the wedding of Juliet
to Paris. Paris arrives to marry Juliet.

Scene Five 152
In Juliet's room, the Nurse finds Juliet, who
looks dead. All are grief-stricken. Friar Laurence
and Paris arrive for the wedding, which will
now be a funeral.

ACT FIVE

Thursday
Scene One 158
In a different city, Mantua, where Romeo has
been living, Romeo's servant Balthasar brings
word that Juliet is dead. Romeo goes to buy
poison to kill himself.

Scene Two 162

In Friar Laurence's cell, Friar John tells Friar Laurence he couldn't deliver the letter telling Romeo about their plan. When he learns this, Friar Laurence goes immediately to the churchyard where Juliet has been placed in the Capulet family tomb.

Friday

Scene Three 164

That night in the churchyard, Romeo and Paris fight. Paris is killed. When Romeo enters the tomb, he sees Juliet, who looks dead. Friar Laurence arrives too late to stop Romeo, who takes the poison. Juliet wakes up. Friar Laurence tries to get Juliet to leave, but she won't. Friar Laurence panics and leaves. Juliet uses Romeo's knife to kill herself.

The Prince arrives. Friar Laurence is caught and tells what happened. Too late to save their children, the Capulets and Montagues call a peace and say they will make gold statues of Romeo and Juliet. Peace and order is brought to the city, but too late for Romeo and Juliet.

Vocabulary words appear in boldface type and are footnoted. Specialized or technical words and phrases appear in lightface type and are footnoted.

Background

William Shakespeare lived and wrote near the end of a time in European history known as the Renaissance, which lasted from 1485 to 1660. The word *renaissance* means "rebirth." During this time, there was a rebirth of interest in the arts and sciences of the classical Greeks and Romans. Like other writers of his time, Shakespeare retold very old stories. *Romeo and Juliet* is one of these old stories.

The Story of *Romeo and Juliet*

A boy and a girl from families that are enemies meet and fall in love. There can be no happy ending. This story has been told over and over. Writers have used the story to show how wasteful fighting and warfare can be.

The first time this story was told was in the writings of a Greek writer named Xenophon. The story that Shakespeare used first appeared in an Italian romance in 1476. The story was then rewritten in French. Then an Englishman named Arthur Brooke wrote it in a long poem called *The Tragical History of Romeo and Juliet* in 1562. Shakespeare wrote his play in the late 1590s.

▲
A theater of Shakespeare's time.

Shakespeare's Theater

The Globe theater was built in 1599 in a small town outside London called Southwark. It was an outdoor summer theater. In 1613 the theater burned down. It was rebuilt in 1614 but was torn down in 1644. However, in London today, Shakespeare's plays are performed in a newly built Globe theater. Now, as in the old times, when the flag is flying over the Globe, a play is going on.

The Globe theater was round and had no roof. It's stage stuck out into the audience. As many as 2,000 people attended the plays, and most of them stood on the ground around the stage. There were three audience balconies with seats that were covered. The most expensive seats were on the shady side.

The stage had doors on either side. There was a small curtain-covered room at the back of the stage and two balconies above it. Juliet stood on the first balcony in the famous balcony scene in Act Two, Scene Two. The second balcony was for the musicians, whose music was like a sound track for the play. Above the stage was a ceiling painted to look like the sky. It was held up by two columns. Above the ceiling was a special effects room. There cannons were fired for the battle scenes. (One of these cannons set off the fire in 1614.) The stage also had a trap door that could be used for magical appearances.

In the play you will find stage directions, for example [*They fight.*]. These tell the actors what to do.

There were no lights in the theater. Plays were presented in the day. There was no scenery, except for a table or chair. Scene changes were very fast, and there were beautiful and expensive costumes.

▲

Shakespeare's coat of arms. (two versions) Originally, a coat of arms really was a coat. Important families each had their own. It was decorated with special designs in and around a shield and often had a family motto on it. Today, a "coat of arms" refers altogether to the shield, the piece above the shield, the figures on its sides, and the motto. Shakespeare's includes an eagle, a pen, oak leaves, and the motto; *Non sans droiet,* or "not without rights."

Shakespeare's Language

Poetry

Shakespeare wrote his plays in verse. Some of itdoes not rhyme and some of it does. The meter, or rhythm of the language, is what makes it poetry. Shakespeare's poetry is in ten-syllable lines with alternating stresses. This kind of verse is called "iambic pentameter." For example:

> *My only love sprung from my only hate!*
> *Too early seen unknown, and known too late.*

In the retelling given here, poetry is not used. However, some of Shakespeare's most famous lines have been included. A note will tell you when three or more lines are exactly as Shakespeare wrote them.

Imagery

In Act Two, Scene Two, Romeo sees Juliet standing in a window with a light behind her. When Shakespeare has him ask, "What light through yonder window breaks ?" and answer his own question, "It is the east and Juliet is the sun," he is using language to build an image of dawn. Shakespeare makes great use of imagery all through his plays.

Puns and Other Fun with Words

Shakespeare loved to have fun with language. He enjoyed jokes. He liked words and phrases that have more than one meaning. In the footnotes, *Wordplay* will point out some of these. Shakespeare's writing shows off the many meanings that a single statement can have. In the opening scene of *Romeo and Juliet*, two servants are kidding with each other. Their speeches are examples of Shakespeare's fun with words.

The Characters

The Capulets

Capulet—Juliet's father; enemy of the Montagues

Lady Capulet—Capulet's wife and Juliet's mother

Juliet—the heroine of the play; Capulet's daughter

Nurse—a servant who has been nurse to Juliet since her birth

Tybalt—Lady Capulet's nephew; Juliet's cousin

Cousin Capulet—a cousin of Juliet's father

Peter—a servant who assists the Nurse

Sampson—a servant

Gregory—a servant

Anthony—a house servant

Potpan—a house servant

Rosaline—Capulet's niece; doesn't appear in the play but is mentioned often

◀ Mercutio

Tybalt ▶

urse

Others

Prince Escalus—the Prince of Verona, Italy

Paris—a count, or nobleman, in the Prince's court; related to the Prince

Page—Paris's servant

Friar Laurence—priest to both Romeo and Juliet; member of the Order of St. Francis

Friar John—a member of the same group of priests as Friar Laurence

Apothecary—like a pharmacist; he makes and sells medicines

Chorus—one or more actors who speak as a group and tell the audience about the play

The Montagues

Montague—Romeo's father; enemy of the Capulets

Lady Montague—Montague's wife and Romeo's mother

Romeo—the hero of the play; Montague's son

Mercutio—Romeo's best friend; also related to the Prince of Verona

Benvolio—Montague's nephew; Romeo's friend and cousin

Abram—Montague's servant

Balthasar—Romeo's servant

Friar Laurence ▶

The Plot

Act One
An old feud between
the Montagues
and the Capulets is
on-going. Romeo, a
Montague, and Juliet,
a Capulet, fall
in love.

Act Two
Romeo and Juliet
marry in secret.

Act Three
Juliet's cousin Tybalt
kills Romeo's best frien
Mercutio. In a flash of
anger, Romeo kills Tybal
Romeo is banished. Julie
father says she must
marry Paris.

Clima:

Rising Action

Begining

ct Four

...et takes a drug
...at makes her seem
... be dead. She is put
... the family tomb.

Falling Action

Act Five

Romeo goes to the
tomb, kills Paris who is
also there, sees Juliet,
and takes poison. Juliet
wakes up, sees Romeo
dead, stabs herself
and dies. The three
bodies are found. The
grieving parents end
the feud.

End

▲
William Shakespeare

Shakespeare's Life

Birth

Shakespeare was born in Stratford-upon-Avon, a small town about seventy-five miles northwest of London, England. His father, John Shakespeare, was a glove maker who owned a shop in Stratford and was elected to local government offices. Shakespeare's mother, Mary Arden, came from a farming family. Shakespeare was baptized on April 26, 1564, a few days after his birth. He was the third of eight children.

Childhood

Shakespeare went to school in Stratford. This was at a time when most people did not get an education and could neither read nor write. His school day was nine hours long. Shakespeare's education gave him the background for much of his writing. In fact, he took many of his ideas for his history plays from a common schoolbook of the time, Holinshed's *Chronicles.*

Stratford was an excellent place to grow up. The town was surrounded by woods, fields, and farms. It was a market town where people came to buy and sell goods. It was very busy, and Shakespeare had a chance to meet and observe many different types of people. During holidays,

COURTESY THE BRITISH LIBRARY

▲
Stratford

popular plays were performed. Traveling companies of actors visited the town, and there were two large fairs every year.

Marriage

In November 1582, at the age of eighteen, Shakespeare married Anne Hathaway, who was twenty-six. Their daughter Susanna was born in May 1583. Twins, Hamnet, a boy, and Judith, a girl, were born in 1585.

Queen Elizabeth I ▶

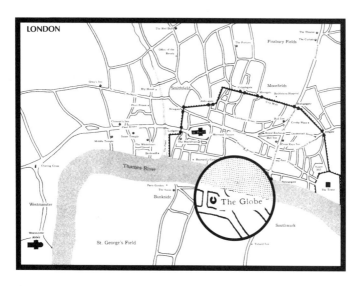

▲
Map of London

London

Seven years after the twins were born, Shakespeare was in London. He worked in the theaters—first in small jobs, then as an actor, and finally as a writer of plays. In 1599, he and six others became owners of the new Globe theater. Queen Elizabeth I supported Shakespeare's company. James I, who became king in 1603, gave the company a royal license. After that, it was known as the King's Men. The company often presented plays for the royal court.

Writing

Shakespeare's first plays were like those of another very popular author, Christopher Marlowe. As Shakespeare wrote more, he developed his own style. He wrote thirty-seven plays in all. His success came in part because he knew firsthand how audiences behaved and what they wanted. He gave audiences exciting stories. He provided funny moments in the midst of tragedies and tragic moments in the middle of comedies. He knew how easily audiences got bored and restless. He made sure there were surprises, magic events, songs, fights, love scenes, and jokes in all his plays.

The years 1592 to 1594 were times of great sickness and disease. The bubonic plague hit London then, and the theaters were often closed. Then Shakespeare turned to writing poems. He wrote two, long, story-telling poems based on Greek mythology, *Venus and Adonis* (1593) and *The Rape of Lucrece* (1594). He also wrote a collection of 154 of the fourteen-line poems known as sonnets.

Later Years

Shakespeare's work brought him fame and money. In 1597, he bought himself a very large house called New Place in Stratford. He moved into it in 1610, spending more and more of his time there. His last play was *The Tempest,* in which a magician who has lived on a deserted magical island returns to his own land after he breaks his magical staff. Shakespeare seems to have gone on helping to write and fix other people's plays after he stopped writing his own. He died in 1616 and was buried in the church at Stratford.

▲
This is what New Place probably looked like during Shakespeare's ownership.

A Shakespeare Time Line

1564—William Shakespeare is baptized on April 26.

1582—He gets a license to marry Anne Hathaway in November.

1592—He is living in London. His first plays have been performed.

1592–1594—The bubonic plague spreads to London. Theaters close. Shakespeare turns to writing poetry.

1596—*Romeo and Juliet* is first performed.

1599—Shakespeare and six others buy the Globe theater.

1603—Queen Elizabeth I dies. The king of Scotland becomes James I of England.

1610—Shakespeare writes his last play, *The Tempest.*

1616—William Shakespeare dies on April 23.

octone

In Shakespeare's time, a group of actors called the Chorus spoke their lines together. Today these lines would probably be spoken by one actor.

It was common for plays to start with a prologue. Also, Shakespeare's audience was very noisy! The prologue gave them time to quiet down. It helped to get their attention. And it helped them understand the play.

[*Enter* Chorus.]

Chorus. In the Italian city of Verona, where this story takes place, two powerful families let an old **feud**[1] start up again. Innocent people will be killed. The guilt for their deaths will be on everyone in the city. From these two feuding families, a pair of star-cross'd lovers[2] take their

---

[1] **feud**—quarrel or fight between two families, often lasting for years.

[2] star-cross'd lovers—the fate of the lovers was predicted by the position of the stars on the day they were born.

lives.[3] Their pitiful adventures fail, and with their death their parents' quarrel dies. The fearful story of their death-marked love and their parents' fight is the two-hour story of this play. If you are patient, what we have not told here, we will show you now.

[*Exit.*]

---

[3] take their lives—*Wordplay:* When Shakespeare says they "take their lives" from the two families, he is making a play on words. This phrase means both "are born" and "commit suicide."

In a public place in Verona, Italy, early one morning, Prince Escalus stops a fight between the Montagues and Capulets and says if any other fights start, he will put the fighters to death. Romeo is sad because he loves a woman who doesn't love him.

[*Enter* Sampson *and* Gregory, *armed with swords and shields. They are servants who work for the Capulet family, which has a long-standing feud with the Montague family.*]

Sampson. Gregory, I promise you no one is going to make us carry coals.[1]

Gregory. No, for then we'd be colliers.[2]

---

[1] carry coals—to do low, dirty work. Sampson means he won't be insulted.

[2] *Wordplay:* In the next three speeches, Sampson and Gregory are playing with words that·sound the same but have different meanings. Colliers—people who carry coal; in choler—angry; collar—hangman's noose.

Sampson. I mean, if we be in choler, we'll draw swords.

Gregory. Yes, while you live, you'll always be drawing your neck out of a collar.

Sampson. I move quickly, if I'm moved[3] at all.

Gregory. But you're not quickly moved to move quickly.

Sampson. A dog from the Montague family moves me.

Gregory. To move is to run away, and to be brave is to stand: therefore, if you are moved, you run away.

Sampson. A dog of the Montague family shall move me to stand.

Gregory. Draw your sword. Here come some of Montague's servants.

[*Enter* Abram *and* Balthasar.]

Sampson. My sword is ready. Fight, I will back you.

Gregory. How, by turning your back and running?

Sampson. Don't be afraid—I'm here!

---

[3] moved—excited or provoked. *Wordplay:* Sampson and Gregory are teasing each other by using words that have more than one meaning.

Gregory. I'm afraid because you are here.

Sampson. Let's keep the law on our side: let them start the fight.

Gregory. I will frown as I pass them, and let them take it as they will.

Sampson. No, as they dare.[4] I will bite my thumb[5] at them, which is a disgrace if they take it.

[Sampson *bites his thumb at* Abram.]

Abram. Do you bite your thumb at us, sir?

Sampson. I do bite my thumb, sir.

Abram. Do you bite your thumb at us, sir?

Sampson. [*Aside*[6]—*whispering to* Gregory] Is the law on our side if I say yes?

Gregory. No.

Sampson. [*Speaking to* Abram] No, sir, I do not bite my thumb at you, sir, but I bite my thumb, sir.

Gregory. Do you wish to quarrel, sir?

Abram. Quarrel, sir? No, sir.

---

[4] dare—have the courage. He also means "accept the challenge."

[5] bite my thumb—an insulting motion made by putting the thumbnail under the upper front teeth, pulling it out, and making a slight click.

[6] **Aside**—a stage direction. It means that the actor should seem to be whispering to another character or thinking out loud to himself.

Sampson. But if you do, sir, I am the man for you. I serve as good a man as you.

Abram. No better.

[Sampson *is confused by this answer. He expected fighting words.*]

Sampson. Well, sir.

[*Enter* Benvolio.[7]]

Gregory. [Gregory *sees* Benvolio, *a Montague, who will fight on their side.*] Say "better"; here comes one of my master's relatives.

Sampson. Yes, better, sir.

Abram. You lie.

Sampson. Draw your sword if you are men. Gregory, remember your swashing[8] blow.

Benvolio. Stop, fools! You don't know what trouble you're causing.

[*Enter* Tybalt, *a Capulet. He wants to continue the feud between the two families.*]

---

[7] Benvolio's name means "good." He's a good guy. He wants to avoid trouble, to stop the fight.

[8] swashing—smashing, forceful slashing.

Tybalt. What, have you drawn your sword on these heartless hinds[9] without a male to protect them? Turn around, Benvolio, and look on your death.

Benvolio. I am just keeping the peace. Put up your sword, or use it to help me stop these men from fighting.

Tybalt. What, you draw your sword and talk of peace? I hate the word "peace," as I hate hell, all Montagues, and you. Fight, coward.

[*They fight.*]

[*Enter three or four citizens with clubs and nine-foot-long spears. The citizens try to stop the fighting. Everyone is sick of the fighting except* Tybalt.]

Citizens. [*They are all shouting.*] Help! Stop them. Knock them down! Down with the Capulets! Down with the Montagues!

[*Enter* Capulet *in his sleeping clothes. His wife,* Lady Capulet, *quickly follows him in.*]

Capulet. What's happening? What's all this noise? Give me my long sword, now!

---

[9] heartless hinds—female deer (hinds) without a male deer (a hart). *Wordplay:* Abram and Sampson are being called "heartless," suggesting they are without enough heart to really put up a brave fight.

Lady Capulet. Call for a crutch! You're too old for a sword!

[*Enter* Montague *and* Lady Montague.]

Capulet. My sword, I say! Old Montague is here, and draws his sword to dare me!

Montague. You're evil, Capulet! [Lady Montague *tries to keep her husband from joining the fight.*] Don't try to hold me! Let me go!

Lady Montague. You won't take one step to seek a **foe!**[10]

[*Enter* Prince Escalus, *the ruler of the city of Verona, with all the people who travel with someone of his importance.*]

Prince Escalus. Enemies to peace. Be quiet! Listen! You men, you beasts! You cool the fire of your rage in fountains of your own blood! Stop or face torture! Throw your bloody weapons to the ground! Hear my judgment on you all. Three public fights have started from nothing but words. Old Capulet and Montague, your families have three times disturbed the quiet of our streets. You've made our old and peaceful people take up weapons of war and broken our

---

[10] **foe**—enemy.

peace with hate! If you ever disturb our streets again, you shall die! For now, everyone leave. You, Capulet, shall go with me. And, Montague, come to see me this afternoon. Once more, leave now or die!

[*Exit all except* Montague, Lady Montague, *and* Benvolio.]

Montague. Who started this old quarrel again? Speak, nephew, were you near when it started?

Benvolio. Your servants and the servants of your enemy were about to fight when I saw them. I drew my sword to part them; at that moment the angry Tybalt arrived, with his sword drawn. He attacked. I defended. More people joined in, fighting on both sides. Then, the Prince arrived and stopped everyone.

Lady Montague. Where is Romeo? Have you seen him today? I am so glad he was not at this fight.

Benvolio. Madam, an hour before dawn I could not sleep and took a walk by the sycamore trees.[11] I saw your son, but he saw me and hid from me. I did not want to see him. He did not

---

[11] sycamore trees—large trees often linked to lovers.

want to see me. I gladly stayed away from Romeo, who gladly ran from me.

Montague. Many a morning he has been seen there in tears till the sun rises. Then he hides himself in his darkened room. I need good advice to find the cause.

Benvolio. My noble uncle, don't you know the cause?

Montague. I don't know the cause, and he won't tell me.

Benvolio. You've asked him?

Montague. I have asked him, and friends have asked him. But he keeps his problems a secret. If I knew the problem, perhaps I could help find a cure for his sorrow.

[*Enter* Romeo.]

Benvolio. Here he comes. Please, go on, I'll find out his problem.

Montague. It would be great luck if you could hear him confess his problem. Come, madam, let's go.

[*Exit* Montague *and* Lady Montague.]

Benvolio. Good morning, Cousin.

Romeo. Is the day so young?[12]

Benvolio. It is just now nine o'clock.

Romeo. Sad hours seem long. Was that my father who left so fast?

Benvolio. It was. What sadness lengthens Romeo's hours?

Romeo. Not having that which, if I had it, would make them seem short.

Benvolio. In love?

Romeo. Out.

Benvolio. Of love?

Romeo. Out of her love who I am in love with.

Benvolio. Sad that love that looks so sweet should be so rough.

Romeo. Sad that love that is blind should still be able to find me. Where shall we eat? [*Romeo sees the evidence of the fight.*] Wait! Was there a fight here? Wait! Don't tell me because I have heard it all. Here is much to do with hate, but more to do with love.[13] Why, then, O fighting

---

[12] day so young—Romeo got up so early it seems late to him. Also, he's lost track of time.

[13] We will soon see that Romeo is in love with a Capulet. No, not Juliet, but her cousin, Rosaline. Romeo knows about the fight between his family and the Capulets, but he also knows he loves a Capulet.

love, O loving hate. Everything is first created out of nothing. O heavy lightness, serious foolishness, misshaped **chaos**[14] of beautiful shapes. Feather of lead, bright smoke, cold fire, sick health! Still-waking sleep that is not what it is! This love feel I, that feel no love in return.[15] Don't you want to laugh at me?

Benvolio. No, coz,[16] I'd rather cry.

Romeo. Good heart, at what?

Benvolio. At your heart's sadness.

Romeo. That's what love does. Your sadness for my sadness makes my sadness grow. Love is a smoke; being made pure, it is a fire sparkling in lovers' eyes; being upset, it is a sea fed with lovers' tears. What else is it? A cautious madness, bitter enough to choke and sweet enough to keep. Farewell, my coz.

Benvolio. Wait, I will go with you. If you leave me this way, you do me wrong.

Romeo. No, I have lost myself. I am not here. This is not Romeo. He's some other place.

---

[14] **chaos**—state of total confusion.

[15] Romeo loves a woman who does not love him.

[16] coz—cousin. In Shakespeare's time, it could mean an actual cousin, a more distant member of the family, or a friend.

Benvolio. Tell me seriously,[17] who is it you love?

Romeo. What, shall I groan and tell you?

Benvolio. Groan? No. But seriously tell me who.

Romeo. Tell a sick man seriously to make his will? A bad thing to say to someone who is sick. Seriously, cousin, I love a woman.

Benvolio. I aimed near[18] when I guessed you loved.

Romeo. You're a beautiful shot; and she that I love is beautiful.

Benvolio. A beautiful target is easiest to hit.

Romeo. Well, you miss because she'll not be hit with love's arrow. She is wearing armor to protect her from love's arrow. She will not let love or lovers' eyes conquer her. Gold cannot win her; she is rich in beauty, only poor because when she dies, her wealth will die with her, as she leaves no children to live after her to show her beauty.

Benvolio. Then she has promised that she will not marry?

---

[17] seriously—without joking, but also sadly.

[18] I aimed near—Benvolio talks about aiming because Cupid, the Roman god of love, shot arrows at people he wanted to fall in love.

Romeo. She has, and what a waste! What beautiful children she would have. She is too beautiful, too wise, to make me so sad. She has promised not to love, and it kills me that I live to tell it now.

Benvolio. Be ruled by me, forget to think about her.

Romeo. Teach me how I can forget to think.

Benvolio. By setting your eyes free: look at other beauties.

Romeo. It will just make me think more of her. When beautiful women wear ugly masks to costume dances, the masks, being ugly, remind us of the beauty they hide. He who has become suddenly blind cannot forget the treasure of his lost eyesight. Show me a girl who is passing fair.[19] Her beauty is just a note to remind me where I may read about the woman who passes that passing fair. Farewell, you cannot teach me to forget.

Benvolio. I'll keep trying to teach you till I die.

[*They exit.*]

---

[19] passing fair—very beautiful, exceedingly (surpassingly) beautiful.

When they meet on a street, Paris tells Juliet's father, Capulet, that he wishes to marry Juliet. Capulet objects because she is too young but says he would allow the marriage when she is older. Capulet invites Paris to a party so that he can see Juliet. Romeo learns about the party and decides to go since Rosaline will be there.

[*Enter* Capulet, Paris, *and a* Servant.]

Capulet. Montague, like me, must keep the peace or suffer the punishment of the Prince. It shouldn't be hard, I think, for men as old as we are to keep the peace.

Paris. You are both good men, and it's a pity you've been at odds for so long. But now, my lord, what do you think of my suit?[1]

---

[1] suit—marriage proposal. Count Paris wishes to marry Capulet's daughter Juliet.

Capulet. As I said before, my daughter is young: she is not yet fourteen years old. Let two more years pass before she becomes a bride.

Paris. Girls younger than she are already happy mothers.

Capulet. And often hurt. I have buried all my children except for her. But try to gain her love, gentle Paris; get her heart. You must get her love before you get my approval. Tonight I am having a party. I have invited many friends; you must be there. All the pleasures that a young man enjoys will be there, including many beautiful young girls. See them all. My daughter will be there. See what you think. Come with me. [*He calls to a* Servant.] You, here are invitations to the party. Deliver these. The names are written on them.

[*Exit* Capulet *and* Paris.]

Servant. Deliver these. The names are written here. And the shoemaker should work with his tape measure, and the tailor with his hammer, the fisherman with his pencil, and the painter with his nets. I am sent to find those persons whose names are written here, but I can never find what names the writing person has written here. I must find someone who can read, and quickly.

[*Enter* Benvolio *and* Romeo.]

Benvolio. Listen, man, one fire burns out another's fuel. One pain is made less by another pain. One grief disappears when another arrives. A new infection cures the old infection.[2]

Romeo. A small bandage will do.[3]

Benvolio. For what?

Romeo. For a broken **shin.**[4]

Benvolio. Are you mad?

Romeo. Not mad, but **confined**[5]: more than a madman is shut up in prison, kept without my food, whipped and beaten . . . [*The* Servant *has been trying to get Romeo's attention. Romeo finally sees him.*] Good evening, good fellow.

Servant. God give you a good evening. I beg you, sir, can you read?

Romeo. Yes, if I know the letters and the language.

[Romeo *is joking with the* Servant, *who thinks* Romeo *is serious.*]

Servant. A good honest answer. Well, be merry.

---

[2] Benvolio is trying to suggest remedies for love—mostly another love.

[3] Romeo is not going to take Benvolio's suggestions seriously.

[4] **shin**—the front part of the leg from knee to ankle.

[5] **confined**—locked up.

Romeo. Stop, I can read.

[*He reads the names on the invitation list.*]

"Signor Martino and his wife and daughters; Count Anselm and his beautiful sisters; the widow of Utruvio; Signor Placentio and his lovely nieces; Mercutio and his brother Valentine; Mine uncle Capulet, his wife and daughters; My fair niece Rosaline and Livia; Signor Valentio and his cousin Tybalt; Lucio and lively Helena."

A very fine group. Where should they go?

Servant. Out.[6]

Romeo. Where are they going?

Servant. To our house.

Romeo. Whose house?

Servant. My master's.

Romeo. I should have asked you that before.

Servant. Now I'll tell you without asking. My master is the great rich Capulet, and if you're not a Montague, I ask you to come and crush[7] a cup of wine. Rest you merry!

---

[6] The Servant isn't as stupid as Romeo thought. The Servant is now teasing Romeo.

[7] crush—drink.

[Servant *exits.*]

Benvolio. Rosaline will be at this party. Rosaline whom you love, with all of the other beauties of this city. Go to this party and fairly compare her face with some I will show you, and I will make you think your swan is a crow.[8]

Romeo. When the worship of my eyes is so false, then may my tears turn to fire, and these eyes which have often drowned may burn for lying. A woman more beautiful than my love! The sun never saw her match since the world began.

Benvolio. You thought her beautiful, when no one else was around: herself being compared with herself in each of your eyes. But weigh her in the scales of your eyes with another girl that I will show you at this party, and she will barely look good who now seems best.

Romeo. I'll go with you, no such sight to be shown, and I'll rejoice in the beauty of my Rosaline.

[*They exit.*]

---

[8] your swan is a crow—the woman you think is as beautiful as a swan will look as ugly as a crow.

At the Capulets' house, Lady Capulet and the Nurse tell
Juliet that Paris wishes to marry her. Juliet agrees to give Paris
a chance, even though she shows little interest in him.

[*Enter* Lady Capulet *and* Nurse.]

Lady Capulet. Nurse, where's my daughter? Call
her to me.

Nurse. I told her to come. Come, lamb. Come,
ladybird. God forbid! Where is she? Come, Juliet.

Juliet. What's the matter? Who calls?

Nurse. Your mother.

Juliet. Madam, I am here. What is your wish?

Lady Capulet. This is the matter.—Nurse, leave
for a while. We must talk in secret.—Nurse,
come back again. I have remembered myself,

you will hear everything we say anyway. You have known my daughter since she was very young.

Nurse. Faith, I can tell her age to the hour.

Lady Capulet. She's not fourteen.

Nurse. I'll bet fourteen of my teeth—but to my sorrow, I have but four teeth—she's not fourteen. How long is it now to Lammastide?[1]

Lady Capulet. Two weeks and a few odd days.

Nurse. Even or odd, when Lammas night comes, she will be fourteen. Susan[2] and she—God rest all Christian souls—were the same age. Well, Susan is with God; she was too good for me. But as I said, on Lammas Eve at night, she will be fourteen. That she will; marry,[3] I remember it well. Since the earthquake, it has been eleven years. We were sitting in the sun by the birdhouse. My lord and you were then at Mantua[4]— I remember. Then the birdhouse shook. I didn't need a second warning. And since that time it has been eleven years. Then she could stand

---

[1] Lammastide—August 1, Juliet's birthday. Lammastide was an early English church harvest festival for the first ripe grain, which was made into loaves of bread and used in the church service.

[2] Susan—the Nurse's own daughter who died at birth.

[3] marry—an expression similar to "indeed." It could indicate surprise, agreement, or indignation.

[4] Mantua—another Italian city nearby.

alone and waddle all about. The day before she hurt her forehead in a fall, and—

Lady Capulet. Enough of this. I pray you, be quiet.

Nurse. Yes, Madam, yet I cannot help but laugh. She was crying, and she suddenly stopped to say. . . .

Juliet. And you should stop, I beg you, Nurse.

Nurse. Peace, I have finished. God give you grace. You were the prettiest baby. If I live to see you married, I will be happy.

Lady Capulet. Marry, that "marry" is the very subject I came to talk of. Tell me, daughter Juliet, how do you feel about being married?

Juliet. It is an honor I have not dreamed of.

Nurse. An honor. Yes, an honor!

Lady Capulet. Well, think about marriage now. Here in Verona, highly regarded ladies, younger than you, are already mothers. I was your mother at about your age. In brief, the bold Paris seeks you for his love.

Nurse. What a man, young lady. Lady, such a man as all the world—why, he's a man of wax.[5]

---

[5] man of wax—an ideal man.

Lady Capulet. Summer doesn't have such a flower.

Nurse. Yes, he's a flower, a perfect flower.

Lady Capulet. What do you say, can you love the gentleman? Tonight you will see him at our party. Read young Paris's face like a book and find delight written there with beauty's pen. Examine every line and see how each will make you happy; and what is hard to read in this book find written in his eyes. Speak briefly, can you like Paris's love?

Juliet. I'll look at him to like him, if looking makes liking, but I'll look no more than you let me.[6]

[*Enter a* Servant.]

Servant. Madam, the guests have come, supper is served, you are called, my young lady is asked for, the nurse cursed in the pantry,[7] and everything is in confusion. I must return to work. Please come quickly.

Lady Capulet. We will follow you. Juliet, the Count Paris waits for you.

[*They exit.*]

---

[6] Juliet will try to like Paris because her mother wishes it.

[7] the nurse cursed in the pantry—Food is stored in the pantry. The Nurse is probably cursed because she has the keys, and they can't get the food without her.

In a street outside the Capulets' house, Romeo and his friends are on the way to the Capulets' party. Romeo explains that he is anxious because of a bad dream. Mercutio teases him by telling him about the fairy Queen Mab who gives dreams.

[*A street.*]

[*Enter* Romeo, Mercutio, Benvolio, *with several young men wearing masks[1] and some carrying torches.*]

Romeo. Shall we give the usual speech?[2] Or shall we enter without it?

Benvolio. That's old-fashioned. We won't have someone introduce us. Let them think what they will. We'll give them a dance and be gone.

---

[1] Young men could attend a party without being invited if they wore a mask. Capulet, who is giving the party, mentions the good times he had going uninvited in a mask to parties when he was young.

[2] usual speech—The young men were expected to give a short speech saying nice things about their host.

Romeo. Give me the torch. I don't feel like dancing. I am so heavy[3] I will carry the light.

Mercutio. No, gentle Romeo, we must have you dance.

Romeo. Not I, believe me. You have dancing shoes with nimble soles. I have a soul of lead that fastens me to the ground.

Mercutio. You are a lover. Borrow Cupid's wings[4] and fly with them above sorrow.

Romeo. I am too wounded with Cupid's arrow to fly with his light feathers, and, so bound,[5] I cannot bound above sadness. Under love's heavy burden I sink.

Mercutio. Love is a tender thing.

Romeo. Is love a tender thing? It is too rough, too rude, too wild, and it pricks like a thorn.

Mercutio. If love be rough with you, be rough with love. Give me a mask to hide my face: a mask for my mask. What do I care what curious eyes see how ugly I am?

---

[3] heavy—sad.

[4] Cupid's wings—Cupid was pictured with wings and a bow and arrow.

[5] so bound—*Wordplay*: Romeo is so tied up (bound) with sorrow he cannot bound (jump) above sorrow.

Benvolio. [*Trying to break the tension.*] Come, knock and enter. When we get in, we'll start a dance.

Romeo. Give me the torch. Let you wild ones tickle the floor with your dancing feet. I'll look on and enjoy the show. I leave the game of love when it is best.[6]

Mercutio. We'll pull you from the mud of love, in which you are stuck up to the ears. Come, we waste the daylight.

Romeo. No, that's not so. It's night.

Mercutio. I mean, sir, we delay. We waste our lights for no reason.

Romeo. We mean well in going to this party, but it's not wise to go.

Mercutio. Why, may one ask?

Romeo. I dreamed a dream tonight.

Mercutio. And so did I.

Romeo. Well, what was yours?

Mercutio. That dreamers often lie.[7]

---

[6] leave . . . when it is best—stop doing something when it is most fun.

[7] dreamers often lie—Mercutio is making fun of Romeo for believing that dreams are warnings.

Romeo. In bed asleep, while they dream things true.

Mercutio. O then I see Queen Mab[8] has been with you. She delivers dreams for the fairies. She comes in shape no bigger than a ring stone on the forefinger of an **alderman,**[9] drawn with a team of little atomies[10] over men's noses as they lie asleep. Her chariot is an empty hazelnut made by the carpenter squirrel. And in this state Mab rides night by night through lovers' brains, and then they dream of love; over courtiers'[11] knees, and they dream of bowing; over lawyers' fingers and they dream of fees; over ladies' lips, and they dream of kisses, and the angry Mab often gives them blisters because they have bad breath. Sometimes she comes with a little pig's tail, tickling a greedy minister's nose as he lies asleep; then he dreams of getting more money. Sometimes she drives over a soldier's neck, and then he dreams of cutting foreign throats, of breaks in walls, attacks, ambushes, Spanish swords, of drinking deep; and then she quickly drums in his ear, at which he jumps and

---

[8] Queen Mab—the fairy in charge of delivering dreams.

[9] **alderman**—a member of the city government.

[10] atomies—small animals, or creatures, as small as an atom.

[11] courtiers'—belonging to the nobles who stay with the king's or queen's court. Courtiers must flatter and bow to the king or queen.

wakes, and being frightened swears a prayer or two and sleeps again. This is the very Mab that tangles the manes of horses in the night and bakes the dirty hair on dirty heads. This is she—

Romeo. Peace, peace, Mercutio, peace. You talk of nothing.

Mercutio. True, I talk of dreams, which are the children of an idle brain, born of nothing but worthless fantasy, which is as thin of meaning as the air and more changing than the wind, who blows on the frozen north now, and, being angered, puffs away from there, turning to the dew-dropping south.

Benvolio. This wind you talk of blows us from our way; supper is done, and we shall arrive too late.

Romeo. I fear too early, for I have doubts. Something will begin with tonight's party. But He that steers my course will direct my way. On, gentlemen.

Benvolio. Strike the drum.[12]

[*They exit.*]

---

[12] Strike the drum—begin to play music. This is an order to the musicians to play while the scene changes.

Inside the Capulets' house during the party, Romeo and Juliet meet and fall in love. Tybalt tries to fight Romeo, but Capulet stops him.

[*The party.* Servants *are hurrying around.*]

First Servant. Where's Potpan?[1] Why isn't he helping us take away and scrape the trenchers?

Second Servant. Good manners don't lie in his hands, and dirty hands too.

First Servant. Take away the stools, remove the cupboard, look to the plates. Save me a piece of candy, and you, tell the porter to let in Susan Grindstone and Nell[2]—Anthony—Potpan!

Second Servant. I'm ready.

---

[1] Potpan—a servant who is supposed to be helping clear the wooden plates that were called trenchers.

[2] Susan Grindstone and Nell—women servants, perhaps invited for a servants' party with the leftovers from the main party.

First Servant. You have been looked for, and called for, asked for and sought for, in the main room.

Second Servant. We cannot be here and there too. Cheerily, boys! Be quick awhile, and the one who lives longest gets everything.

[*The* Servants *exit.*]

[*Enter* Capulet, Lady Capulet, Juliet, Tybalt, Nurse, *many* Guests.]

Capulet. Welcome, gentlemen. Ladies who don't have corns[3] on their toes will dance with you. Ah my ladies, which of you will refuse to dance now? She that won't dance I'll swear has corns. Am I right? Welcome, gentlemen.

[Capulet *welcomes the masked young men, including* Romeo.]

I have seen the day that I have worn a mask to a party and could whisper a story in a lady's ear that would please her. That time is gone. It's gone. You are welcome, gentlemen. Come, musicians, play. Clear the dance floor, give room! And dance it, girls!

---

[3] corns—a painful hardening or thickening of the skin, especially on a toe. They are not very romantic or glamorous.

[*Music plays, and they dance. Shakespeare's plays, even the serious and sad ones, have music and dancing.*]

[*To the* Servants] More light, you knaves,[4] and move the tables. Put out the fire, the room is too hot. [*To his* Guests] Ah, this unplanned dancing is fun. No, sit, sit, good cousin Capulet. You and I are past our dancing days. How long is it since you and I wore masks at a party?

Cousin Capulet. By our Lady,[5] thirty years.

Capulet. What, man, it's not so long, it's not so long. It was at the marriage of Lucentio. It's twenty-five years: and then we wore the masks.

Cousin Capulet. It's more, more. His son is older, sir: his son is thirty.

Capulet. Will you tell me that? His son was just a child two years ago.

[Romeo *comes to the front of the stage. He sees* Juliet. Romeo *is instantly in love with* Juliet, *attracted by her beauty.*]

---

[4] knaves—servants.

[5] by our Lady—in the name of Mary, the mother of Jesus. Cousin Capulet is showing he is serious.

Romeo. [*To a* Servant] What lady is that who does enrich the hand of yonder knight?[6]

Servant. I know not, sir.

[Tybalt *overhears* Romeo *and recognizes him.*]

Romeo. O, she doth teach the torches to burn bright!
It seems she hangs upon the cheek of night
As a rich jewel in an Ethiop's[7] ear—Beauty too rich for use, for earth too dear!
So shows a snowy dove trooping with crows
As yonder lady o'er her fellows shows.[8]

The dance done, I'll watch where she stands, and touching her hand make blessed my rough hand. Did my heart love till now? Swear it is not true, sight. For I never saw true beauty till this night.

[Tybalt *and* Capulet *come to the front of the stage.*]

Tybalt. This by his voice should be a Montague. Get my sword, boy. How dare he come here, covered with a party mask, to mock and scorn

---

[6] yonder knight—that man over there.

[7] Ethiop's—belonging to a person from Ethiopia. A jewel would stand out against black skin.

[8] The previous six lines are in Shakespeare's original language.

our festival? Now, by the honor of my family, it will not be a sin to kill him.

Capulet. What are you doing, kinsman? Why do you look so angry?

Tybalt. Uncle, this is a Montague, our foe: a **villain**[9] who wishes to ruin our party.

Capulet. Is it young Romeo?

Tybalt. It's him, that villain Romeo.

Capulet. Be quiet, gentle coz, let him alone. He acts like a gentleman; and, to tell the truth, people say he is a good youth. I would not for the wealth of all this town treat him badly in my house.[10] Therefore be patient, do not notice him. It is my command. If you respect me, smile, stop frowning, and do not make a stir. You are showing a poor face for a party.

Tybalt. A frown is the right face when such a villain is a guest. I'll not put up with him.

Capulet. You shall put up with him. What, boy! I say you shall! Go to,[11] am I the master here or you? Go to. You'll not put up with him! God

---

[9] **villain**—a wicked person.

[10] Even Capulet doesn't seem to want to keep the feud going.

[11] Go to—do what I say. Capulet doesn't like people to disobey him. He has a short temper.

help my soul, you'll make a fight among my guests, you'll have things your way! You'll be the man!

Tybalt. Why, uncle, it's a shame.

Capulet. Go to, go to. You are childish. It is a shame? I'll teach you a lesson. I know you! You always go against me. It's time you stopped arguing and fighting—[*To the party* Guests] Well done, my friends—[*To* Tybalt] You are a spoiled child. Go, be quiet, or—[*To the* Servants] More light! More light!—[*To* Tybalt] For shame, I'll make you quiet—[*To the party* Guests] What, be cheerful, my hearts!

Tybalt. [*To himself*] I am patient with his anger, but it makes me angry. I will leave, but if Romeo thinks it sweet to be here now, it will be sour soon.

[Romeo *now has our attention. He touches* Juliet's hand.]

Romeo. If I insult with my unworthiest hand this holy shrine, the gentle sin is this: my lips, two blushing pilgrims, ready stand to smooth that rough touch with a tender kiss.[12]

---

[12] Romeo has touched Juliet on the hand. He says he will kiss her hand to make up for his rude touch.

Juliet. Good pilgrim, you do insult your hand too much. Your good-mannered devotion shows this way; for saints have hands that pilgrims' hands do touch, and palm to palm is holy palmer's kiss.[13]

Romeo. Don't saints have lips, and holy palmers too?

Juliet. Yes, pilgrim, lips that they must use in prayer.

Romeo. O then, dear saint, let lips do what hands do: they pray. Say yes, or my faith will turn to despair.

Juliet. Statues of saints do not move though they grant prayers.

Romeo. Then don't move while my prayer is answered.

[*He kisses her.*]

Thus from my lips, by your lips, my sin is removed.

Juliet. Then do my lips have the sin they took from your lips?

---

[13] holy palmer's kiss—Juliet says he is very holy, like a palmer, someone who has been to the land where Christ lived. These religious pilgrims would pray by putting their palms together. She suggests this is like hands kissing.

Romeo. Sin from my lips? O sin sweetly asked for. Give me my sin back.

[*He kisses her again.*]

Juliet. You kiss by the book.[14]

Nurse. Madam, your mother wants to speak with you.

[Juliet *goes to her mother.*]

Romeo. Who is her mother?

Nurse. Marry, bachelor, her mother is the lady of the house, and a good lady, and wise and virtuous. I nursed her daughter that you talked with. I tell you, he that can get hold of her shall be rich.

Romeo. Is she a Capulet? O terrible accounting.[15] My life is owed to my enemy.

Benvolio. Away, be gone. The party is at its best.

Romeo. Yes, so I fear; the more is my unrest.

Capulet. No, gentlemen, don't leave. We have a light refreshment.

---

[14] kiss by the book—Juliet is teasing Romeo. She says he kisses like he learned it in a book. She is asking for a more passionate kiss.

[15] O terrible accounting—Romeo is saying he has a terrible new debt in his accounts. He owes his life (Juliet) to his enemy (the Capulets).

[*They whisper in his ear. They are giving an excuse for leaving. Perhaps they are saying they have another party to go to, or people to meet.*]

Is that so? Why, then, I thank you all. I thank you, honest gentlemen. Good night. More torches here. Come on then. Let's go to bed. Ah, it gets late. I'll go to my rest.

[*Everyone starts to leave except* Juliet *and the* Nurse.]

Juliet. Come here, Nurse. Who is that gentleman?[16]

Nurse. The son and heir of old Tiberio.

Juliet. Who is he that is now going out the door?

Nurse. Marry, that I think is young Petruchio.

Juliet. Who is he that follows, who did not dance?

Nurse. I don't know.

Juliet. Go ask his name.

[*The* Nurse *leaves to find out* Romeo's *name.*]

If he be married, my grave will be my marriage bed.[17]

---

[16] that gentleman—Juliet is asking about other men to hide her interest in Romeo from the Nurse.

[17] my grave will be my marriage bed—This is a tragedy. This innocent remark is really a clue to what will happen.

[*The* Nurse *returns.*]

Nurse. His name is Romeo, and a Montague, the only son of your great enemy.

Juliet. My only love sprung from my only hate!
Too early seen unknown, and known too late.
Prodigious[18] birth of love it seems to me,
That I must love a hated enemy.[19]

Nurse. What's this? What's this?

Juliet. A rhyme I learned just now from one I danced with.

[*Someone calls* Juliet *from off stage.*]

---

[18] Prodigious—amazing (in a bad sense), monstrous.
[19] Juliet's speech is in Shakespeare's original words.

act two

Outside the Capulet's house. Romeo's friends, Benvolio and Mercutio, try to find him, but he hides from them.

[*Enter* Chorus.]

Chorus. Now old love lies in his death bed, and young love longs to be his heir. Rosaline's beauty, which Romeo groaned for and would die for, is now not beauty compared to Juliet's. Now Romeo is loved and loves again. Both Romeo and Juliet are bewitched by the charm of looks. Now he must love his supposed foe, and Juliet must steal love's sweet bait from frightening hooks. Being called a foe, he may not whisper such vows as lovers use; and she, as much in love, is even less able to meet her new love anywhere. But passion lends them power, time lends them a way to meet, and extreme hardships are softened by extreme sweetness.

[*Exit.*]

[*Enter* Romeo *alone. Outside the Capulets' enclosed garden.*]

Romeo. Can I go somewhere else when my heart is here? Turn back, dull earth,[1] and find your center.

[Romeo *hides. Enter* Benvolio *with* Mercutio.]

Benvolio. Romeo! My cousin, Romeo! Romeo!

Mercutio. He is wise and has gone home to sleep.

Benvolio. He ran this way and jumped over this wall. Call, good Mercutio.

Mercutio. I'll **conjure**[2] too: Romeo! Moody! Madman! Passion! Lover! Appear in the likeness of a sigh, speak but one rhyme, and I am satisfied. Cry out, 'I'm sad!' Say just 'love' and 'dove.' Say to my old friend Venus[3] just one word. Give one nickname for her blind son Cupid, he that shoots so well. Romeo doesn't hear, doesn't stir, doesn't move: the ape is

---

[1] dull earth—Romeo's body, whose center is Juliet.

[2] **conjure**—magically call up a spirit. Mercutio tries to call Romeo, using different names: for example, madman, lover.

[3] Venus—the goddess of love.

dead,[4] and I must conjure him. I conjure you by Rosaline's[5] bright eyes, by her high forehead and her scarlet lip, by her fine foot that you appear to us.

Benvolio. If he hears you, he will be angry.

Mercutio. This cannot anger him. It would anger him if I called up a spirit and his lady had to do away with it. That would be mean. My calling is fair and honest. I only use his lady's name to call him.

Benvolio. Come, he has hidden among these trees to be with the sad night. Blind is his love and fits best with the dark.

Mercutio. If love be blind, love cannot find its target. Now he will sit under a tree and wish he were with her, wish she were his. O Romeo, I wish she were. Romeo, good night. I'll go home to my little bed. Sleeping outside is too cold for me. Shall we go?

Benvolio. Let's go. It's no good hunting a person who doesn't want to be found.

[*Exit* Benvolio *and* Mercutio.]

---

[4] the ape is dead—in a circus trick, a monkey would pretend to be dead.

[5] Mercutio uses Rosaline's name to call up Romeo. Mercutio doesn't know yet that Romeo now loves Juliet.

Outside the Capulets' house, under Juliet's balcony, Romeo overhears Juliet confess her love for him. Romeo tells Juliet he loves her. Juliet sets up a plan for their marriage.

[Romeo *comes forward.*]

Romeo. [*To himself*] He jests at scars that never felt a wound.[1]

[*Enter* Juliet *on the balcony.*]

But soft![2] What light through yonder window
    breaks?
It is the east and Juliet is the sun!
Arise, fair sun and kill the envious moon,[3]
Who is already sick and pale with grief
That thou her maid are far more fair than she,

---

[1] He jests at scars—a person who has never felt a pain laughs when someone else has a pain. Mercutio laughs because he's never been in love.

[2] But soft!—quiet!

[3] Romeo compares Juliet to the rising sun and says she is more beautiful than the moon.

Be not her maid, since she is envious,

Her vestal livery[4] is but sick and green,

And none but fools do wear it. Cast it off.

It is my lady; O, it is my love!

O, that she knew she were!

She speaks, yet she says nothing. What of that?[5]

Her eye speaks. I will answer it.

I am too bold. It is not to me she speaks.

Two of the fairest stars in all the heaven,

Having some business, do beg her eyes

To twinkle in their place till they return.

What if her eyes were there, and the stars were
    in her head?

The brightness of her cheek would shame
    those stars

As daylight shames a lamp. Her eyes in heaven

Would through the sky stream so bright

That birds would sing and think it were not
    night.

See, how she leans her cheek upon her hand.

O that I were a glove upon that hand,

That I might touch that cheek.

Juliet. O, me.

---

[4] vestal livery—clothes worn by servants of the moon, virginal.

[5] The first eleven lines of Romeo's speech are in Shakespeare's original language. A long uninterrupted speech is called a *soliloquy*. This soliloquy is very famous, and the whole scene is one of the most famous scenes in all literature.

Romeo. [*To himself*] She speaks. O speak again, bright angel, for you are as glorious to this night, being over my head, as is an angel from heaven to the upturned eyes of **mortals**[6] who fall back to look at him when he rides on the lazy clouds and sails on the air.

Juliet. [*To herself*] O Romeo, Romeo, wherefore art thou Romeo?[7]
Deny your father and refuse your name. Or if you will not, promise your love to me, and I'll no longer be a Capulet.

Romeo. [*To himself*] Shall I listen more, or shall I speak at this?

Juliet. [*To herself. She still doesn't know* Romeo *is there.*] It is your name that is my enemy: you are yourself, even if you changed your name from Montague. What's Montague? It is not hand or foot or arm or face or any other part belonging to a man. O, be some other name. What's in a name? That which we call a rose by any other name would smell as sweet; so Romeo would, if he were not called Romeo, keep that dear perfection which he owns

---

[6] **mortals**—normal people who will die, not gods.

[7] Wherefore art thou Romeo?—Juliet isn't asking where Romeo is. She is asking why he is Romeo, a member of the family that her family hates.

without that name. Romeo, give up your name, and for your name, which is no part of you, take all of me.

Romeo. [*To* Juliet] I take you at your word. Just call me love, and I'll be new baptized: from now on I never will be Romeo.

Juliet. What man are you that is hidden by the night and hears my private words?

Romeo. By a name I know not how to tell you who I am: my name, dear saint, is hateful to me because it is an enemy to you. If my name was written on a piece of paper, I would tear it up.

Juliet. My ears have not yet drunk a hundred of your words, yet I know the sound. Aren't you Romeo, and a Montague?

Romeo. Neither, fair maid, if you dislike either.

Juliet. How did you come here, tell me, and for what reason? The garden walls are high and hard to climb, and the place death, considering who you are, if any of my kinsmen[8] find you here.

Romeo. With love's light wings did I fly over these walls, for stone walls cannot hold love out. And

---

[8] kinsmen—family.

what love can do, love dares to do: therefore, your kinsmen cannot stop me.

Juliet. If they see you, they will murder you.

Romeo. Alack, there lies more **peril**[9] in your eye than in twenty of their swords. Look but sweet, and I am protected against their hatred.

Juliet. I would not for all the world have them see you here.

Romeo. I have night's cloak to hide me from their eyes, and if you don't love me, let them find me here. My life was better ended by their hate than to live if you do not love me.

Juliet. Who helped you find this place?

Romeo. Love, that first made me ask where you were. He gave me advice, and I loaned him eyes. I am no pilot, yet, if you were as far as the farthest shore washed with the farthest sea, I should search after such a treasure.

Juliet. You know that night covers my face, or a maiden blush would paint my cheek for that which you heard me speak tonight. Gladly would I be more formal; gladly, gladly deny what I have spoken. But farewell, modesty. Do

---

[9] **peril**—danger.

you love me? I know you will say "Yes," and I will believe you. Yet, if you swear that you love me, you may lie. At lover's lies, they say, Jove[10] laughs. O gentle Romeo, if you do love me, say it truly. Or if you think I am too quickly won, I'll frown and say no to you, so you will woo me; but otherwise, I would not frown at you for the world. In truth, fair Montague, I am too fond of you; therefore, you may think me too easily won, but trust me, gentleman, I'll prove more true than those who pretend to be less interested. I should have pretended to be less interested, I confess. But you overheard me speak my true love's passion before I knew you were there; therefore, pardon me, and don't think this is a light love which the dark night has allowed you to discover.

Romeo. Lady, I swear by the blessed moon, that tips with silver all these fruit-tree tops—

Juliet. O, don't swear by the moon, not the moon, that monthly changes her shape, or your love may also prove changeable.

Romeo. What shall I swear by?

---

[10] Jove—the most important Roman god. He had many love affairs, and he lied to his wife about them.

Juliet. Do not swear at all. Or if you must, swear by your kind self, which is the god I worship, and I'll believe you.

Romeo. If my heart's dear love—

Juliet. Well, do not swear.[11] Although I have joy in you, I have no joy in what we are doing: it is too fast, too poorly thought out, too much without advice, too sudden, too much like lightning, which is over before you can say that it is lightning. Sweet, good night! This bud of love, during the warmth of summer, may grow into a flower when we meet again. Good night, good night. As much sweet peace and rest come to your heart as there is in mine.

Romeo. O will you leave me so unsatisfied?

Juliet. What satisfaction can you have tonight?

Romeo. The exchange of your promise of love for mine.

Juliet. I gave you mine before you asked for it. And yet, I wish I could give it again.

Romeo. Would you take it back? Why, love?

---

[11] Juliet keeps interrupting Romeo, possibly because she doesn't want him to say the practiced, common words that lovers said.

Juliet. Only to be generous. I would take it back, so I could give it to you again; and yet I wish only for what I have.

My bounty[12] is as boundless as the sea,

My love as deep; the more I give to thee.

The more I have, for both are **infinite.**[13]

I am coming soon, good Nurse—Sweet Montague, be true to me. Stay here; I will come back quickly. I hear a noise inside. Dear love, adieu.[14]

[*The* Nurse *calls from off stage.*]

[Juliet *exits.*]

Romeo. O blessed, blessed night. I am afraid, since it is night, that I am dreaming. This is too flattering and sweet to be real.

[*Enter* Juliet *on the balcony.*]

Juliet. Quickly, dear Romeo, then really good night. If your love is honorable and your purpose marriage, send me word tomorrow of where and when we will be married,[15] and all I have is yours. I'll follow you throughout the world.

---

[12] bounty—generosity.

[13] **infinite**—everlasting. These three lines are in Shakespeare's original words.

[14] adieu—French word for "goodbye."

[15] This is all very fast. They met earlier in the day. Now Juliet is planning on marrying Romeo the next day.

Nurse. [*Out of sight*] Madam.

Juliet. [*To the* Nurse] I will come in a moment. [*To* Romeo] But if you don't mean well, I beg you—

Nurse. Madam.

Juliet. [*To the* Nurse] I am coming right away— [*To* Romeo] I beg you to stop this, and leave me to my grief. Tomorrow I will send someone to bring your message.

Romeo. So thrive[16] my soul—

Juliet. A thousand times good night.

[*Exit* Juliet.]

Romeo. A thousand times worse, to miss your light. Love goes toward love as schoolboys go away from their books, but love leaves love as schoolboys go to school, with heavy looks.

[*Enter* Juliet *on the balcony, again.*]

Juliet. Hist![17] Romeo, hist! [*To herself*] O, for a falconer's voice,[18] so I could call back my falcon. I cannot speak loudly, or I will be heard. If I

---

[16] thrive—flourish, prosper. Juliet is Romeo's soul. He wishes her to thrive, to do well.

[17] Hist—listen.

[18] A falconer trained hunting birds. If allowed to fly free, the birds would return when the falconer called them.

could, I would shout so loud I would destroy the cave where Echo[19] lies and make her more hoarse than me with repeating my Romeo's name.

Romeo. It is my soul that calls my name. How silver-sweet lovers' voices sound at night. Like the most beautiful music.

Juliet. Romeo.

Romeo. My dear?

Juliet. What time tomorrow shall I send the message to you?

Romeo. Nine o'clock.

Juliet. I will not fail. It will seem like twenty years until then. I have forgotten why I called you back.

Romeo. Let me stand here until you remember.

Juliet. I shall keep forgetting, so I can have you stand there, remembering how I love you to be with me.

Romeo. And I will stay here to have you forget, forgetting any other home but this.

---

[19] Echo—in Greek mythology, a young girl who fell in love, but whose love was not returned. She faded away until nothing was left but her voice. She lived in lonely places, such as caves.

Juliet. It's almost morning. You must leave. And yet I don't want you to go farther than a little girl's pet bird, hopping from hand to hand like a poor prisoner, and with a silken thread I would pull you back again. I am so loving-jealous of your freedom.

Romeo. I wish I were your bird.

Juliet. Sweet, so would I.
Yet I should kill you with much cherishing.[20]
Good night, good night! Parting is such sweet sorrow
That I shall say good night till it be morrow.[21]

[*Exit* Juliet.]

Romeo. Sleep be on your eyes, peace in your breast. I wish I were sleep and peace to have so sweet a place to rest! I will go to Friar Laurence to ask his help and tell him of my happiness.

[*Exit* Romeo.]

---

[20] cherishing—loving care.
[21] morrow—tomorrow.

In Friar Laurence's cell in the monastery, the Friar agrees to marry Romeo and Juliet because he sees a chance to stop the feud between the two families.

[*Enter* Friar Laurence *alone. He carries a basket.*]

Friar Laurence. The grey-eyed morning smiles on the frowning night, splashing the eastern clouds with streaks of light. Now before the sun cheers up the day and dries night's dew, I will fill this basket with weeds and healing flowers. From the earth where we bury the dead comes new life. And we, earth's children, find much that we can use in what earth gives us. All plants have some use, and all are different. There are many powerful gifts that lie in plants and stones. For nothing is so bad that it can't do some good; nothing so good but if misused may be bad. Virtue turns into vice if misused, and vice sometimes by doing good is good.

[*Enter* Romeo.]

Within this flower is poison and medicine's power: being smelled, it makes a person feel better; being tasted, it stops the heart. Two such opposite powers are in man as well as in a flower: love and selfishness; and where the worse is stronger, soon the worm, death, eats up the plant.

Romeo. Good morning, Father.

Friar Laurence. Blessings, my son. Young son, something must be wrong for you to be up so early. Care makes old men get up early. But where young men lie down, there sleep should come easily. Therefore, your earliness tells me something is wrong. If that's not it, then now I will hit it right: our Romeo has not been in bed tonight.

Romeo. The last is true. The sweeter rest was mine.

Friar Laurence. God pardon sin. Were you with Rosaline?

Romeo. With Rosaline! My father, no. I have forgotten that name and that name's sorrow.

Friar Laurence. That's my good son. But where have you been?

Romeo. I'll tell you before you ask me again. I was with my enemy where suddenly one of them wounded me and was wounded by me.[1] You may cure us both. I bear no hatred, blessed Father, for when you help me, you help my foe.

Friar Laurence. Be plain, good son, confusing confession brings confusing forgiveness.[2]

Romeo. Then plainly know that my heart is set on the fair daughter of rich Capulet. As my love has been given to her, so hers has been given to me. All that's missing is for you to bring us together in holy marriage. When and where, and how we met, we grew to love each other, and gave each other our vows, I'll tell you as we go; but this I pray, say you will marry us today.

Friar Laurence. Holy Saint Francis! What a change is here! Is Rosaline that you loved so much so soon left? Young men's love then lies not really

---

[1] Romeo and Juliet were wounded by love.

[2] confusing forgiveness—Friar Laurence doesn't understand what Romeo is talking about.

in their hearts but in their eyes. Jesu Maria! What a lot of **brine**[3] has washed your cheeks for Rosaline. How much salt water is wasted to season love that you then don't taste. The sun has not cleared your old sighs away. Your old groans still ring in my old ears. Look, here on your cheek the stain still sits from an old tear that is not washed off yet. All of these sorrows were for Rosaline. Have you changed? Here is a new saying then: Women may fall when there's no strength in men.

Romeo. You often scolded me for loving Rosaline.

Friar Laurence. For thinking you loved, not for loving, my pupil.

Romeo. And you told me to bury love.

Friar Laurence. Not in a grave, to put one in and pull another out.

Romeo. I pray you, don't scold me. The woman I love now loves me back. The other didn't.

Friar Laurence. O, she knew well that you didn't know any more about love than children who can't spell. But come, come with me. In one way

---

[3] **brine**—salt water. Many tears are shed in love, and then it turns out you don't love.

this marriage may be good—it may turn your two families' hatred into love.

Romeo. O, let us go quickly.

Friar Laurence. Let us go wisely and slowly; they fall who run too fast.

[*Exit* Romeo *and* Friar Laurence.]

On a public street, Tybalt challenges Romeo to fight. Romeo tells the Nurse his plan to marry Juliet that afternoon. The Nurse will take a rope ladder to Juliet so that Romeo may climb to her balcony that night.

[*Enter* Benvolio *and* Mercutio.]

Mercutio. Where the devil is Romeo? Did he come home last night?

Benvolio. No, I spoke with his servant.

Mercutio. Why, that pale hard-hearted wench,[1] that Rosaline, torments him so that he will go mad.

Benvolio. Tybalt, a kinsman to old Capulet, has sent a letter to Romeo.

---

[1] wench—a young woman, a servant. The use of this term shows disrespect for Rosaline.

Mercutio. A challenge,[2] I'll bet.

Benvolio. Romeo will answer it.[3]

Mercutio. Any man that can write may answer a letter.

Benvolio. No, he will answer the letter's writer that he dares to fight, being dared to fight.

Mercutio. Alas, poor Romeo, he is already dead, stabbed with a woman's eye, run through the ear with a love song, the very center of his heart shot through with an arrow from Cupid's bow. Is he in any shape to fight Tybalt?

Benvolio. Why, what is Tybalt?

Mercutio. More than Prince of Cats.[4] He fights very carefully and by the book. One, two, and the third in your chest: he butchers silk buttons. He is a duelist,[5] a duelist! He has taken the finest lessons, and knows all the causes for fighting. He knows all the sword thrusts well.

Benvolio. All of them?

---

[2] challenge—demand for a duel.

[3] answer it—accept the challenge.

[4] Prince of Cats—Tybalt was the name given in English children's stories to the Prince of Cats.

[5] duelist—person who fights another person with deadly weapons.

Mercutio. A curse on these showoffs! This Tybalt is a very good fighter, a brave man. I dislike him much! It is a sad thing that we should be bothered by him.

[*Enter* Romeo.]

Benvolio. Here comes Romeo!

Mercutio. Made worse by the ladies. Now he knows what the love poems mean. Signor Romeo, good day. You gave us the slip last night.

Romeo. Pardon, good Mercutio, I had important business, and in such a case a man may be a little discourteous.

Mercutio. I am the very pink[6] of courtesy.

Romeo. Pink for flower.

Mercutio. Right.

Romeo. Why, then my shoe is covered with flowers.

Mercutio. Come between us, good Benvolio, my **wits**[7] fail.

Romeo. Use the switch and spurs on your wits to get them to run faster, or I'll claim I beat you!

---

[6] pink—*Wordplay:* Mercutio likes to make puns. "Pink" can mean "very good," "a flower," or "decorative hole in a shoe."

[7] **wits**—sense or thinking ability.

Mercutio. Why, isn't this better than complaining about love? Now you are good company, now you are the real Romeo; for love makes you like a big idiot running around.

[Romeo *sees the* Nurse *and her servant,* Peter. *They are both wearing very fancy clothes.*]

Romeo. Here comes some noble clothing.

Benvolio. A sail! A sail!

Mercutio. Two. Two—A shirt and a dress.

Nurse. Peter.

Peter. Here.

Nurse. My fan, Peter.

Mercutio. Yes, Peter, to hide her face, for her fan looks better than her face.

Nurse. Good morning, gentlemen.

Mercutio. Good evening, fair gentlewoman.

Nurse. Is it evening?

Mercutio. It is past noon.

Nurse. Who are you?

Romeo. A man, gentlewoman, that God made to ruin himself.

Nurse. Well said. Gentlemen, can any of you tell me where I may find young Romeo?

Romeo. I can tell you; but young Romeo will be older when you have found him than he was when you looked for him. I am the youngest of that name, for lack of a worse.

Nurse. You say well.

Mercutio. Is the worst well?

Nurse. If you are Romeo, sir, I need to speak to you in private.

Benvolio. She will invite him to supper.

Mercutio. A wild woman! A wild woman! Romeo, will you come to your father's house? We're going to dinner there.

Romeo. I will follow you.

Mercutio. Farewell, ancient lady. Farewell, [*singing*] lady, lady, lady.[8]

[*Exit* Mercutio *and* Benvolio.]

Nurse. Pray you, sir, a word—My young lady told me to find you. What she told me to say, I will keep to myself for now. But first let me tell you, if you should trick her, that would be very bad;

---

[8] lady—Mercutio is singing a song about a loose woman to tease the Nurse about her morals.

for the gentlewoman is young. And therefore, if you should trick her, truly it were a bad thing to do to any gentlewoman, a very weak thing to do.

Romeo. Nurse, recommend me to your lady. I protest to you—[9]

Nurse. Good heart, I will tell her. Lord, Lord, she will be a joyful woman.

Romeo. What will you tell her, Nurse? You didn't let me finish.

Nurse. I will tell her, sir, that you do protest—which, as I understand it, means you "declare your love" for her.

Romeo. Tell her to find some way to come to the church this afternoon, and there at Friar Laurence's cell she shall be married. Here is something for your pains.

[Romeo *tries to give the* Nurse *some money.*]

Nurse. No, truly, sir; not a penny.

Romeo. Yes, take it. I say you shall.

Nurse. This afternoon, sir? Well, she shall be there.

---

[9] I protest to you—*Wordplay:* Romeo is going to "protest," to complain to the Nurse because she has suggested that he might hurt Juliet. The Nurse thinks he is going to "protest," solemnly promise to marry Juliet.

Romeo. And, good Nurse, wait behind the church wall. Within an hour, my servant shall be with you, and bring a rope ladder. It will be my way to your lady in the secret of the night. Farewell, be trusty, and I'll reward your pains. Farewell. Recommend me to your lady.

Nurse. Now, God in heaven bless you! Listen, sir.

Romeo. What, dear Nurse?

Nurse. Can your servant keep a secret? Did you ever hear the saying, "Two may keep a secret if only one knows it"?

Romeo. I know my man can be trusted.

Nurse. Well, sir, my mistress is the sweetest lady— Lord! Lord!—O, there is a nobleman in town, named Paris, that would like to marry my lady; but she would rather see a toad than see him.

Romeo. Recommend me to your lady.

[*Exit* Romeo.]

Nurse. Yes, a thousand times. Peter!

Peter. Yes.

Nurse. Let's go, quickly.

[*They exit.*]

In the Capulets' orchard, the Nurse tells Juliet about Romeo's plans for their marriage.

[*Enter* Juliet.]

Juliet. It was nine o'clock when I sent the Nurse. She promised to return in half an hour. Perhaps she can't find him. That can't be. O she is slow. Love's messengers should fly ten times faster than sunbeams. She has been gone for three hours and is not back yet. If she loved and was young, she would go as fast as a ball. But many old people act as if they were dead[1]—slow, heavy as lead.

[*Enter* Nurse *and* Peter.]

O, she comes. O honey Nurse, what news? Have you met with him? Send your servant away.

---

[1] Juliet mentions death often.

Nurse. Peter, stay outside.

[*Exit* Peter.]

Juliet. Now, good sweet Nurse—O Lord, why do you look so sad? If your news is sad, tell me merrily. If your news is good, don't shame it with a sour face.

Nurse. I am weary. Let me rest awhile. O, how my bones ache.[2]

Juliet. I wish you had my bones and I had your news. I beg you, speak: good, good Nurse, speak.

Nurse. What a hurry. Can't you wait awhile? Don't you see I am out of breath?

Juliet. How can you say you're out of breath when you have enough breath to say that you are out of breath? The excuse you make is longer than the story you have to tell. Is your news good or bad? Answer that. Say either, and I'll wait for the details. Tell me: is it good or bad?

Nurse. Well, you have made a foolish choice. You don't know how to choose a man. Romeo? No, not he. Though his face is better than any other man, his leg's excellent, and his hand and foot

---

[2] The nurse is teasing Juliet by keeping Romeo's message from her.

and body, though I shouldn't talk about them, they are the best. He is not as courteous as he could be, but he seems as gentle as a lamb. Go your way, girl, serve God. Have you eaten at home?

Juliet. No, no. I knew all of this before. What did he say about our marriage? What of that?

Nurse. Lord, how my head aches! What a headache I have: it feels like my head would fall into twenty pieces. My back, too—ah, my back! You should be ashamed for sending me to run errands in my bad health.

Juliet. I am sorry that you are not feeling well. Sweet, sweet, sweet Nurse, tell me, what says my love?

Nurse. Your love says, like an honest gentleman, and courteous, and kind, and handsome, and I believe virtuous—Where is your mother?

Juliet. Where is my mother? She is inside. How oddly you reply. "Your love says, like an honest gentleman, Where is your mother?"

Nurse. O God's lady dear, are you so anxious? So much in a hurry. Is this the medicine for my pains? From now on do your own errands.

Juliet. What a fuss. Come, what does Romeo say?

Nurse. Have you got permission to go to church today?

Juliet. I have.

Nurse. Then go quickly to Friar Laurence's **cell**.[3] There you will find a husband to make you a wife. Now I see you blush. Get to church. I have to go another way to get a ladder by which your love can climb to your nest when it is dark. I must do the work, so you can have the fun. Go. I'll go to dinner. Get you to the cell.

Juliet. I will go to good fortune! Honest Nurse, farewell!

[*They exit.*]

---

[3] **cell**—small room.

In Friar Laurence's cell, Juliet and Romeo meet to be married by Friar Laurence.

[*Enter* Friar Laurence *and* Romeo.]

Friar Laurence. Let Heaven smile on this holy act, so that we will not regret it in the future.

Romeo. Amen, Amen, but no sorrow can cancel the joy that one short minute with her gives me. Just marry us, then let love-devouring death do what he dares: it is enough to call her mine.

Friar Laurence. These violent delights have violent endings, and in their triumph die, like fire and gunpowder, which, as they kiss, destroy themselves.[1] Honey can be too sweet and

---

[1] When fire and gunpowder "kiss," touch each other, the gunpowder explodes, destroying both the fire and the gunpowder.

make us to lose our appetite. Therefore, love **moderately;**[2] a long lasting love does so. Too fast is just as wrong as too slow.

[*Enter* Juliet *very quickly and embraces* Romeo.]

Here comes the lady. O, so light a foot will never wear out the hard rock under it. A lover may walk upon spider webs and not fall; so light is vanity.[3]

Juliet. Good evening to my spiritual confessor.

Friar Laurence. Romeo shall thank you for us both, daughter.

Juliet. I will thank him.

Romeo. Ah, Juliet, if your joy is as great as mine and you have more skill to describe it, then tell us of the coming happiness that we will receive from this dear meeting.

Juliet. There is more here than I can put into words. My true love has grown so much that I cannot sum up half my good fortune.

---

[2] **moderately**—not extremely.

[3] so light is vanity—so unimportant are the pleasures of this world.

Friar Laurence. Come, come with me, and we will
do this quickly, for I will not leave you alone till
you are married.

[*They exit.*]

act three

*In a public place, Tybalt, Juliet's cousin, tries to start a fight with Romeo. Because Romeo has just married Juliet, he refuses to fight with her cousin. Mercutio fights with Tybalt. When Romeo tries to stop the fight, Tybalt uses the chance to stab Mercutio. Mercutio dies. Romeo kills Tybalt. Romeo is **exiled**.[1]*

[*Enter* Mercutio *and* Benvolio.]

Benvolio. I beg you, good Mercutio, let's leave. The day is hot, which makes tempers bad. The Capulets are near, and if we meet them, there will be a fight.

Mercutio. You wish to fight more than any man I know!

Benvolio. Me?

---

[1] **exiled**—forced to leave his native land, banished.

Mercutio. Why, you will fight with a man who cracks hazelnuts because you have hazel colored eyes. You've quarreled with a man for coughing in the street because he woke up your dog. And yet you try to teach me not to quarrel!

Benvolio. If I were as likely to quarrel as you, I would be dead in an hour and a quarter.

[*Enter* Tybalt *and some of his kinsmen.* Tybalt *is hunting for* Romeo *to fight him because* Romeo *came to the Capulets' party.*]

Benvolio. By my head, here come the Capulets.

Mercutio. By my heel, I care not.

Tybalt. [*Speaking to the other young men with him*] Stay near to me, for I will speak to them. [*He speaks to* Mercutio *and* Benvolio.] Gentlemen, good evening. I would like to have a word with one of you.

Mercutio. Just one word with one of us? Couple it with something. Make it a word and a blow.

Tybalt. You will find me able to do that if you give me the chance.[2]

---

[2] Tybalt doesn't want to fight with Mercutio, who is the better swordsman. Mercutio is also related to the Prince, who has forbidden them to fight.

Mercutio. Couldn't you take a chance without having it given to you?

Tybalt. Mercutio, you consort[3] with Romeo.

Mercutio. Consort? What, do you think we are hired musicians? Here's my fiddlestick.

[Mercutio *draws his sword.*]

This will make you dance.

Benvolio. We are in a public place. Either go somewhere that is private, or work out your problems, or leave. Here everyone can see what you do.

Mercutio. Men's eyes were made to look; let them look. I will not leave to please any man.

[*Enter* Romeo.]

Tybalt. Well, peace be with you, sir. Here comes my man.[4]

Mercutio. But I'll be hanged, sir, if he wears your livery.[5] Ask him to fight, and he will do what you ask. In that sense he is your man.

---

[3] *Wordplay:* consort—hang around with, but Mercutio, who likes to twist words, takes "consort" to mean a group of musicians, which is another meaning of the word.

[4] my man—Romeo. "My man" could also mean "my servant."

[5] livery—servant's clothes.

Tybalt. [*To* Romeo] Romeo, you are a villain.

Romeo. Tybalt, I have reason to excuse your insult. I am not a villain. Therefore, farewell. You do not really know me.

Tybalt. Boy, this doesn't excuse the injuries you have done me. Turn and draw your sword to fight.

Romeo. I never injured you, but have reason to care for you more than you know. And so, good Capulet, which name I value as much as my own, be satisfied.

Mercutio. O calm, dishonorable, vile submission: a good cut with my sword takes this dishonor away.

[Mercutio *draws his sword.*]

Tybalt, you rat-catcher,[6] will you come with me?

Tybalt. What do you want with me?

Mercutio. Good King of Cats, I just want one of your nine lives. If you treat me well, I may let you keep the other eight. Will you draw your sword? Hurry, or mine will be out sooner.

---

[6] rat-catcher—Remember, Tybalt's name was also used for the Prince of Cats in children's stories.

Tybalt. I'm ready to fight.

[Tybalt *draws his sword.*]

Romeo. Gentle Mercutio, put your sword away.

Mercutio. Come, sir, give me your best.

[Tybalt *and* Mercutio *fight.*]

Romeo. Draw your sword, Benvolio. Beat down their weapons. Gentlemen, for shame. Stop this. Tybalt, Mercutio! The Prince has forbidden us to fight on the streets. Stop, Tybalt! Good Mercutio!

[*While* Romeo *is between* Tybalt *and* Mercutio *trying to beat down their swords,* Tybalt *stabs* Mercutio *by thrusting his sword under* Romeo's *arm, a cowardly move. One of the young men with* Tybalt *shouts for him to run away, which* Tybalt *does.*]

Mercutio. I am hurt. A plague on both your houses.[7] I am killed. Has he left without a hurt?

Benvolio. What? Are you hurt?

Mercutio. Yes, yes. A scratch, a scratch. But it's enough. Where is my page? [*To* Page] Go villain, get a doctor.

---

[7] A plague on both your houses—Mercutio knows he has been seriously wounded. He curses both families (both houses) by wishing they have a terrible disaster (plague).

[*The* Page *exits to get a doctor.*]

Romeo. Courage, man, the hurt cannot be much.

Mercutio. No. It's not as deep as a well, nor as wide as a church door, but it's enough. It will do. Ask for me tomorrow, and you will find me a grave man. A plague on both your houses. Zounds,[8] a dog, a rat, a mouse, a cat, he scratches a man to death. A bragger, a villain, that fights by the book—why the devil did you step between us? I was hurt under your arm.

Romeo. I thought I was doing what was best.

Mercutio. Help me into some house, Benvolio, or I shall faint. A plague on both your houses. They have made worm's meat[9] out of me. I have it, and soundly too—your houses!

[*Exit* Mercutio *helped by* Benvolio.]

Romeo. This gentleman, the Prince's near relative, my good friend, has been wounded fighting for me—fighting because Tybalt insulted me— Tybalt who has been my cousin for an hour. O sweet Juliet, your beauty has made me weak and softened my courage.

---

[8] Zounds—cursing. A shortened form of "By God's wounds."

[9] worm's meat—a dead person.

[*Enter* Benvolio.]

Benvolio. O, Romeo, Romeo, brave Mercutio is dead. His spirit has left this earth.

Romeo. This day's sad fate will ruin many more days: this day begins what other days must end.

[*Enter* Tybalt.]

Benvolio. Here comes the furious Tybalt back again.

Romeo. He comes in triumph, and Mercutio is dead. I won't be peaceful now! I must be fiery-eyed.[10] Now, Tybalt, take back the "villain" you called me, for Mercutio's soul is just a little above our heads waiting for your soul to keep him company. Either you, or I, or both must go with him.

Tybalt. You traveled with him here, and now you shall go with him.

Romeo. This shall decide that.

[*They fight. Romeo kills Tybalt.*]

Benvolio. Romeo, away! Run! The citizens are coming, and Tybalt is dead! Don't just stand

---

[10] fiery-eyed—angry.

there. The Prince will have you put to death if they catch you. Get out of here!

Romeo. O, I am fortune's fool.

Benvolio. Why do you stay?

[Romeo *exits. A crowd of armed* Citizens *enter. They are angry at the constant fighting.*]

Citizen. Which way did Mercutio's murderer run? Which way did Tybalt, who murdered Mercutio, run?

Benvolio. There lies that Tybalt.

Citizen. Come with us. I command you to speak to the Prince.

[*Enter the* Prince, Montague, Capulet, *their wives, and a crowd.*]

Prince. Where are the criminals who started this fight?

Benvolio. O noble Prince, I can tell you all that happened. There lies the man, slain by young Romeo, that killed your kinsman Mercutio.

Lady Capulet. [Lady Capulet *is very upset to see her nephew dead.*] Tybalt, my cousin! O my brother's child! O Prince! O cousin! Husband!

O, the blood is spilled of my dear kinsman! Prince, as thou art true, for blood of ours, shed blood of Montague. O cousin, cousin!

Prince. Benvolio, who started this fight?

Benvolio. Tybalt, who was then killed by Romeo. Romeo spoke peacefully to him, tried to talk him out of the quarrel, and told him of your strong displeasure. But Tybalt, deaf to talk of peace, thrust his sword at Mercutio, who fought back. Romeo tried to stop them. He beat down their swords and stood between them. Tybalt thrust his sword under Romeo's arm and killed Mercutio. Then Tybalt ran away, but soon came back to Romeo. Romeo now thought about revenge, and before I could stop them, they fought. Tybalt was killed. Then Romeo fled. This is the truth or let me die.

Lady Capulet. He is a kinsman to the Montague. Affection makes him false; he speaks not true. Some twenty of them fought in this black **strife,**[11] And all those twenty could but kill one life. I beg for justice, which you, Prince, must give. Romeo slew Tybalt; Romeo must not live.

---

[11] **strife**—fight.

Prince. Romeo killed Tybalt. Tybalt killed Mercutio. Who pays for Mercutio's death?

Montague. Not Romeo, Prince. He was Mercutio's friend; he ended what the law would have ended, Tybalt's life.

Prince. And for that crime I exile him immediately. I have a personal interest in this now, for your illegal fights have killed my kin. I will give you such a heavy punishment that you shall repent the loss of my kin. I will be deaf to your begging, excuses, tears, and prayers. Therefore use none. Romeo must leave this city quickly. If my men find him, he dies. Remove Tybalt's body, and do what I have commanded. We encourage murder when we pardon killers.

[*The* Prince *and his men exit, the Capulet men carrying* Tybalt's *body.*]

In the Capulets' orchard, the Nurse tells Juliet that Romeo killed Tybalt. At first Juliet is angry at Romeo, but then she declares her loyalty to Romeo. The Nurse promises to bring Romeo that night.

[*Enter* Juliet *alone.*]

Juliet. Sun, set quickly. Cloudy night, come soon, so Romeo may leap to my arms unseen. Love is blind, so night doesn't matter. Night will hide my shyness.

Come, night; Come, Romeo; Come, thou[1] day in night;

For thou wilt[2] lie upon the wings of night

Whiter than new snow on a raven's back.

Come, gentle night; come, loving, black-browed

---

[1] thou—you.

[2] wilt—will.

night,

Give me my Romeo; and when he shall die,
Take him and cut him out in little stars,
And he will make the face of heaven so fine
That all the world will be in love with night
And pay no worship to the garish[3] sun.

This day is so long. It's like the night before a holiday to an impatient child who has new clothes to wear. O, here comes my Nurse.[4]

[*Enter* Nurse *with the rope ladder. She is wringing her hands.*]

Now, Nurse, what news? What do you have? The rope ladder that Romeo told you to bring to me?

Nurse. Yes, yes, the rope ladder.

Juliet. What news do you have for me? Why are you so upset?

Nurse. Ah, terrible day, he's dead, he's dead, he's dead! He's gone. He's killed. He's dead.[5]

Juliet. Can heaven be so envious?

---

[3] garish—bright, glaring. The nine lines that end with this one are in Shakespeare's original words.

[4] This is another of the most famous speeches in the play.

[5] Confusion is a main theme in this play. Juliet thinks Romeo has been killed. The Nurse means Tybalt has been killed.

Nurse. Romeo can, though heaven cannot. O, Romeo, Romeo—who ever would have thought it? Romeo!

Juliet. What devil are you? Why do you torture me? Has Romeo killed himself? Say yes or no!

Nurse. I saw the wound. I saw it with my eyes— God save me. I saw it right on his chest. A pitiful corpse, a bloody, pitiful corpse. Pale, pale as ashes, all covered with blood. All in blood. I fainted at the sight.

Juliet. O break, my heart. Poor heart, break at once. I will kill myself and be buried with Romeo.

Nurse. O Tybalt, Tybalt, the best friend I had. O good Tybalt, honest gentleman. I wish I hadn't lived to see you dead.

Juliet. What, both dead? Romeo and Tybalt? My dearest cousin and my dearer lord? This is like the end of the world. For who is living if these two are gone?

Nurse. Tybalt is dead, and Romeo is **banished**.[6] Romeo killed Tybalt, and for that, Romeo is banished.

---

[6] **banished**—sent out of the country. He cannot return.

Juliet. Did Romeo shed Tybalt's blood?

Nurse. He did. He did! Alas the day! He did.

Juliet. O **serpent's**[7] heart hid under a flower's face. Beautiful **tyrant**,[8] fiendish angel, dove-feathered raven, wolfish lamb! You are the exact opposite of what you seemed. A damned saint, an honorable villain! O that lies should live in such a gorgeous palace.

Nurse. There's no trust, no faith, no honesty in men. All of them are liars, all. These griefs make me old. Shame come to Romeo.

Juliet. May your tongue be blistered for saying that. He was not born for shame. Shame is ashamed to shame him. O, what a beast I was to be angry with him.

Nurse. Will you speak well of him who killed your cousin?

Juliet. Shall I speak ill of him who is my husband?[9] Ah, poor Romeo, who will comfort you when your wife of three hours has said bad things about you? But why, villain, did you kill

---

[7] **serpent's**—snake's.

[8] **tyrant**—cruel ruler.

[9] Juliet has quickly decided she must be loyal to Romeo, not Tybalt.

my cousin?[10] Because that villain cousin would have killed my husband. Stop, foolish tears. You belong to sad times. My husband lives who Tybalt would have killed. And Tybalt is dead who would have killed my husband. Why do I weep then? There was a word worse than Tybalt's death that made me cry. I wish I could forget it. But O, it stays in my memory like guilt in a sinner's mind. Tybalt is dead, and Romeo is—banished. Banished! That one word, *banished,* is worse than the death of ten thousand Tybalts. Tybalt's death was sad enough, but "Romeo is banished" is like killing father, mother, Tybalt, Romeo, Juliet. Romeo is banished. There is no end, no limit, in that word's sadness. Where is my father and mother, Nurse?

Nurse. Weeping and wailing over Tybalt's corpse. Will you go to them? I'll take you there.

Juliet. Do they wash his wounds with their tears? I will weep longer for Romeo's banishment. Pick up the rope ladder. Poor ladder, you and I have been tricked, for Romeo is exiled. He made this ladder as a highway to my bed. But

---

[10] Although Juliet supports Romeo, she is still upset with the events which happened so quickly. Her feelings are not clear yet.

now I'll die a maiden-widow. I'll go to my wedding bed, and there I'll meet death, not Romeo.

Nurse. Go to your bedroom. I'll find Romeo for you. I know where he is. Listen, your Romeo will be here tonight. I'll get him. He is hiding in Friar Laurence's cell.

Juliet. Find him. Give him this ring, and tell him to come to say his last goodbye.

[*Exit* Juliet *and* Nurse.]

In Friar Laurence's cell, the Friar tells Romeo that the Prince has sent him away. Romeo says that death would be better than being sent away from Juliet. The Nurse arrives to bring Romeo to Juliet. Friar Laurence calms Romeo.

[*Enter* Friar Laurence.]

Friar Laurence. Romeo, come here. Sadness loves you, and you are married to **calamity**.[1]

[*Enter* Romeo.]

Romeo. Father, what news? What has the Prince said?

Friar Laurence. He has not doomed you to death, but to banishment.

Romeo. Ha! Banishment? Be merciful, say "death." Banishment is more terrible than death.

---

[1] **calamity**—disaster or misfortune.

Friar Laurence. You are banished from this city of Verona. Be patient. The world is broad and wide.

Romeo. There is no world outside of Verona but torture and hell.

Friar Laurence. O deadly sin. O rude unthankfulness. By our law you should die, but the Prince has shown mercy. This is mercy, and you don't see it.

Romeo. 'Tis torture and not mercy. Heaven is here, where Juliet lives, and every cat and dog and little mouse, every unworthy thing, live here in heaven and may look on her, but Romeo may not.

A fly may land on Juliet's hand, but Romeo may not see her. He is banished. Flies may do this, but from this I must fly. They are free, but I am banished. Exile is death. Don't you have any poison or a knife to kill me quickly? No, you have a slow "banished" to kill me. O Father, the damned use that word in hell.

Friar Laurence. You foolish madman. Listen to me.

Romeo. O, you will speak again of banishment.

Friar Laurence. I'll give you the armor of philosophy[2] to comfort you, banished though you are.

Romeo. You say it again. Unless philosophy can make a Juliet, relocate a town, reverse the Prince's sentence, it helps me not. Don't talk any more!

Friar Laurence. O, now I see that madmen don't have ears.

Romeo. Why should they when wise men have no eyes.

Friar Laurence. Listen to me.

Romeo. You can't talk about what you don't feel. If you were as young as I am, Juliet your love, an hour married, Tybalt murdered, loving like me, and like me banished, then you could speak. Then you might tear your hair and fall on the ground as I do, thinking of the grave.

[*There is a knock on the door.*]

Friar Laurence. Get up, Romeo. Hide.

Romeo. Not I, unless sorrow covers me and hides me.

---

[2] the armor of philosophy—armor protects, and philosophy is wise thinking. A good philosophy would help protect a person from life's troubles.

[*Another knock.*]

Friar Laurence. Hear how they knock.—Who's there?—Romeo, get up. You will be captured. Get up.

[*Another knock.*]

Run to my study.—I'm coming.—What foolishness is this?—I'm coming. I'm coming.

[*Another knock.*]

Who knocks so hard? What do you want?

Nurse. [*Off stage*] Let me in. I come from Lady Juliet.

Friar Laurence. Welcome then.

[*Enter* Nurse.]

Nurse. O holy Friar, O, tell me, holy Friar, where is my lady's lord? Where's Romeo?

Friar Laurence. There on the ground. His tears have made him drunk.

Nurse. My lady Juliet is the same way. She lies on the floor just like that: blubbering[3] and weeping, weeping and blubbering. Stand up.

---

[3] blubbering—crying without restraint.

Stand up. Act like a man for Juliet's sake. For her sake stand up.

[Romeo *stands up*.]

Romeo. Nurse.

Nurse. Ah sir, death's the end of everything.

Romeo. Are you talking about Juliet? How is she? Does she think of me as an old murderer now that I have ruined these early days of our love with the blood of her cousin? Where is she? How is she? And what does she say about our lost love?

Nurse. O, she doesn't say anything, sir, but weeps and weeps. Then she falls on her bed, then jumps up, and calls for Tybalt, and then calls for Romeo, and then falls on her bed again.

Romeo. Does she call my name as if she hated me? O tell me, Friar, in what part of my body is my name? Tell me that I may destroy it.

[Romeo *draws his dagger*.]

Friar Laurence. Stop thinking such thoughts. Are you a man? You look like one, but you cry like a woman. Your wild actions are like an animal's. You amaze me! I thought you were better. Have you killed Tybalt? Will you kill yourself? That would kill your Juliet. You shame your shape, your love, and your wit. Wake up, man. Your Juliet is alive. There you should be happy. Tybalt wanted to kill you, but you killed Tybalt. There you should be happy. The law that threatened to kill you became your friend and gave you exile instead. There you should be happy. A pack of blessings have fallen on you, but, like a spoiled child, you complain. Listen. Go to your love. Go to her room and comfort her. But don't stay after dawn, or the guards will be after you. Before dawn, go to Mantua, where you will live until we can win back your reputation and get the Prince to pardon you. Go now, Nurse, and try to get everyone to go to bed early. Romeo is coming.

Nurse. O Lord, I could have stayed here all night to hear good advice. O, what learning is! My lord, I'll tell my lady you will come.

Romeo. Do so.

[Nurse *starts to go, but turns back.*]

Nurse. Here, sir, is a ring she told me to give to you. Come quickly, for it is getting late.

Romeo. How this makes me happy.

Friar Laurence. Go, good night. Here is what you must do: Leave town before the day breaks. Leave in disguise. Go to Mantua. I will send your servant with messages to tell how things are going here. Farewell. Good night.

Romeo. Except a greater joy calls to me, I would not leave you. Farewell.

[*They exit.*]

In a room in the Capulets' house, Capulet decides that Juliet should marry Paris on Thursday.

[*Enter* Capulet, Lady Capulet, *and* Paris.]

Capulet. Things have happened, sir, so unluckily that we have had no time to help you win our daughter. She loved her cousin Tybalt dearly, and so did I. Well, we were all born to die. It's very late. She won't come downstairs tonight. And, if you weren't here, I would have gone to bed an hour ago.

Paris. These times of sorrow don't give any time for love. Madam, good night. Remember me to your daughter.

Lady Capulet. I will, and I will see how she feels about you tomorrow. Tonight she is too sad.

[Paris *starts to go inside, but* Capulet *calls to him.*]

Capulet. Sir Paris, I will make a bold promise of my child's love.[1] I think she will do what I ask. I know she will do what I ask. Wife, go to Juliet before you go to bed, and tell her of my son Paris's love, and tell her—are you listening carefully?—on next Wednesday—but wait— What is today?

Paris. Monday, my lord.

Capulet. Monday! Ha, ha! Well, Wednesday is too soon. On Thursday let it be. On Thursday, tell her, she shall be married to this noble lord. [*To Paris*] Will you be ready? Is this too fast? We won't have a big wedding—a friend or two. For listen, since Tybalt was killed so recently, it may be thought we didn't care for him if we celebrate too much at this wedding. Therefore, we'll have perhaps half a dozen friends. That's all. Is Thursday all right?

Paris. My Lord, I wish Thursday were tomorrow.

---

[1] Capulet makes a sudden change here. He tells Paris that Juliet will marry him; although earlier he said Juliet was too young. It is Monday. Watch the time. Everything happens quickly.

Capulet. Well, go then. It soon will be Thursday. Wife, go to Juliet before you go to bed, and tell her to get ready for her wedding day. Good night, my lord Paris. It is so late that we may call it early soon enough. Good night.

[*They exit.*]

Early in the morning, on Juliet's balcony, Romeo leaves. Romeo has been with Juliet through the night. Juliet's mother comes to tell her the new plans for her to marry Paris. When Juliet refuses, Capulet threatens to throw her out if she doesn't obey his wishes. The Nurse tells Juliet to forget Romeo and marry Paris.

[*Enter* Romeo *on Juliet's balcony.*]

Juliet. Are you leaving? It is not yet day. It was the nightingale that sang, not the lark. She sings on that tree every night. Believe me, love, it was the nightingale.[1]

Romeo. It was the lark, who sings in the early morning, not the nightingale. Look, love, see the sun's early light in the east. Night's candles

---

[1] A nightingale sings at night. A lark sings early in the morning. Juliet doesn't want the night to be over because Romeo will have to leave. But if he is caught now, he will be put to death.

are burned out, and happy day stands tiptoe on the misty mountaintops. I must be gone and live, or stay and die.

Juliet. That light is not daylight. I know it. It is some meteor that has come to light your way to Mantua. Please stay a little longer; you don't need to leave yet.

Romeo. Let them find me; let me be put to death. I am happy if you wish it. I'll say that morning is not here. I want to stay more than to go. Come, death, and welcome. Juliet wants it so. How is it, my love? Let's talk. It is not day.

Juliet. It is! It is! Go, begone, away! It is the lark that sings so out of tune. O now be gone, more light and light it grows.[2]

Romeo. More light and light?—more dark and dark our woes.

[*Enter* Nurse, *hastily.*]

Nurse. Madam.

Juliet. Nurse?

Nurse. Your mother is coming to your room.

[Nurse *exits.*]

---

[2] Juliet knows she could put Romeo in danger. She knows he must leave.

Juliet. Then, window, let day in, and let life out.

Romeo. Farewell, farewell, one kiss and I'll leave.

[Romeo *climbs down the ladder.*]

Juliet. Are you gone? My lord, my love, my husband, my friend, I must hear from you every day, every hour. In a minute there are many days.

Romeo. Farewell. I won't miss a chance to send my greetings, love, to you.

Juliet. Do you think we will ever meet again?

Romeo. I know we will. And all these sorrows will just be stories in the future.

Juliet. O God, I am afraid of that future. I think I see you now as if you were at the bottom of a grave.[3] Either my eyes fail or you look pale.[4]

Romeo. Trust me, love, you also look pale. Sorrow drinks our blood. Good-bye.

[Romeo *exits.*]

---

[3] at the bottom of a grave—Romeo is on the ground. Juliet is looking down at him from the balcony as if she were looking down on him in a grave.

[4] There was a belief that sorrow took blood away. Upset people do often look pale.

Juliet. O Fortune, Fortune! You have taken him away, but change your mind and bring him back.

[*Enter* Lady Capulet.]

Lady Capulet. Hello, Juliet, are you up?

Juliet. Who is it that calls? Is it you, mother? Why are you here so late, or up so early? What brings you here?

[Juliet *leaves the balcony. At this point* Juliet *would disappear briefly from the audience's view. When she joins her mother, the stage is her bedroom.*]

Lady Capulet. How are you now, Juliet?

Juliet. Madam, I am not well.

Lady Capulet. Still weeping for your cousin's death? Will you wash him from his grave with your tears? If you could, you could not make him live. Try to stop. Some grief shows much love, but much grief shows lack of wit.

Juliet. Yet let me weep for my loss.

Lady Capulet. Weeping will make you feel the loss, but not the friend you weep for.

Juliet. Feeling the loss, I cannot help weeping.

Lady Capulet. Probably you weep not as much for his death as for the villain who still lives.

Juliet. What villain, madam?

Lady Capulet. Why, that villain Romeo who murdered your cousin Tybalt.

Juliet. Villain who is miles away. [*To herself*] God pardon him. I do with all my heart. [*To* Lady Capulet] And yet no man hurts my heart as much as he.

Lady Capulet. That is because the murderer lives.

Juliet. Yes, madam. He lives far from the reaches of my hand. I wish no one but I could punish him.[5]

Lady Capulet. We will punish him. Then weep no more. I'll send a servant to Mantua, where that banished Romeo lives, and poison him so that he shall keep Tybalt company. Then I hope you will be satisfied.

Juliet. Indeed, I never shall be satisfied until I see him—dead—my poor heart is so troubled for a kinsman.[6] O how my heart hates to hear his name when I cannot go to him.

---

[5] Juliet appears to her mother to hate Romeo, but we see that her mother doesn't really understand Juliet's meaning.

[6] Juliet almost gives herself away with her careless words. This can be read "until I see him dead" or "dead is my poor heart."

Lady Capulet. Find the poison, and I'll find a man to take it. But now, I'll tell you good news.

Juliet. And we need good news in such bad times. What is it?

Lady Capulet. Well, well, you have a father who cares for you, child. A father who in this sadness has found you a day of joy that you don't expect.

Juliet. What day is that?

Lady Capulet. Early next Thursday morning the brave, young, and noble gentleman, the Count Paris, at Saint Peter's Church, shall happily make you his bride.

Juliet. Now, by Saint Peter's Church and Saint Peter himself, he shall not make me a happy bride. Why is he in such a hurry? Should I marry a man who has not come to win me? I beg you tell my father, madam, I will not marry yet. And when I do, I swear it shall be Romeo, whom you know I hate, rather than Paris.

Lady Capulet. Here comes your father, tell him yourself, and see how he will take it.

[*Enter* Capulet *and* Nurse.]

Capulet. When the sun sets, there is dew; but for the sunset of my brother's son, it rains.[7] Girl, are you still crying? Your eyes are like the sea: they flow with tears. Wife, have you told her our wishes?

Lady Capulet. Yes, sir, but she will not do it. She gives you her thanks. I wish the fool were married to her grave![8]

Capulet. What? I don't think I understand you. She will not do it? Doesn't she think herself blessed that we have found her such a man to make her a bride? Is she too proud to have him?

Juliet. Not proud, but thankful. I cannot be proud of what I hate. But I am thankful that what I hate was meant for love.[9]

Capulet. What, what, what? This is strange thinking! What do you mean? "Proud" and "I thank you" and "I thank you not." Thank me no thankings nor proud me no prouds. Get yourself ready, for next Thursday you will go with Paris to Saint Peter's Church, or I will drag

---

[7] Capulet sees Juliet's tears and thinks she is crying for Tybalt.

[8] Lady Capulet says she wishes Juliet were dead. She doesn't, of course, but people, when they are irritated, often say hurtful words that they don't mean.

[9] Juliet hates the idea of marrying Paris even though she is proud her father set up the marriage because he loved her.

you there. Out, you foolish girl! Out, you baggage![10] You tallow-face![11]

Lady Capulet. For shame. Are you mad?

[Capulet *has lost his temper.* Lady Capulet *is trying to stop him.*]

Juliet. Good father, I beg you on my knees.

[Juliet *falls to her knees.*]

Please, let me speak.

Capulet. Hang you, disobedient child! I tell you what—Go to church on Thursday or never see me again. Speak not, reply not, do not answer me. Wife, we thought we were blessed when God gave us a child. But now I see this one child is one too much, and we have a curse in having her. Out of here, wicked girl.

Nurse. God in heaven bless her. You are to blame to scold her.

Capulet. And why, my lady wisdom? Be quiet.

Lady Capulet. You are too angry.

Capulet. It makes me mad! Day, night, work, play, alone, in company, I have always thought of her. Now I have taken care of her with such an

---

[10] baggage—something that's a lot of trouble, but you have to carry it. Sometimes used as a term of endearment, but not here.

[11] tallow-face—pale. Juliet looks sick.

excellent man, and she answers, "I'll not wed. I cannot love. I am too young. I beg you, pardon me!" If you don't marry, go where you want. You will not live here. Think about it. I am not joking. Thursday is near. Consider this: if you are mine, I'll give you to my friend Paris; if you are not mine, hang! Beg! Starve! Die in the streets! For by my soul, I will not recognize you. I'll not help you. Trust me. Think about it.

[Capulet *exits.*]

Juliet. Is there no pity in heaven that sees my grief? O sweet mother, do not throw me out. Delay this marriage for a month, a week, or if you do not, make my bridal bed in the tomb where Tybalt lies.

Lady Capulet. Don't talk to me, for I'll not speak a word. Do as you wish, for I am done with you.

[Lady Capulet *exits.*]

Juliet. O God, O Nurse, how shall this be stopped? I am already married. Help me. Tell me what to do. Why would God do this to one so weak? What do you say? Give me some comfort.

Nurse. Faith, here it is. Romeo is banished, and dares not come back. As things stand, I think it is best for you to marry the Count Paris. O, he's a lovely gentleman. Romeo is nothing compared to him. I think you will be happy in this second match. It's better than the first. Besides, your first marriage is dead, or as good as dead. . . .

Juliet. Do you speak from your heart?

Nurse. And from my soul too, or send them both to hell.

Juliet. Amen!

Nurse. What?

Juliet. Well, you have comforted me much. Go in and tell my mother that since I made my father angry, I am going to Father Laurence's cell to confess and be forgiven.

Nurse. Yes, I will. This is wisely done.

[*The* Nurse *exits.*]

Juliet. Wicked old woman! O most wicked fiend. Is it worse to wish me to swear falsely or to dispraise my lord with the same tongue she used to praise him? Go, my advisor. I'll never love you again.[12] I'll go to the Friar to get his help. If all else fails, I have the power to die.

[*Exit.*]

---

[12] Juliet has been abandoned by everyone, even the Nurse.

In Friar Laurence's cell, Paris is arranging his wedding when Juliet arrives. Juliet threatens suicide if Friar Laurence can't stop the marriage. Friar Laurence suggests a plan to fake Juliet's death so that Romeo and Juliet can be together.

[*Enter* Friar Laurence *and* Paris.]

Friar Laurence. On Thursday, sir? The time is very short.

Paris. My father-to-be wants it so, and so do I.

Friar Laurence. You say you do not know how the lady feels about you? I don't like this.

Paris. She weeps much for Tybalt's death, and so I have not had a chance to win her love. Her father thinks she is too sad and hurries our marriage to cheer her, to take her mind off her sorrow. Now you know why we are in such a hurry.

Friar Laurence. [*To himself*] I wish I did not know why it should be slowed. [*To* Paris] Look, sir, here comes the lady now.

[*Enter* Juliet.]

Paris. I am glad to see you, my lady and my wife.

Juliet. That may be, sir, when I may be a wife.

Paris. That "may be," must be, love, on Thursday next.

Juliet. What must be, shall be.

Friar Laurence. That's for certain.

Paris. Did you come to confess to this holy father?

Juliet. If I answered that, I would be confessing to you.

Paris. Do not deny to him that you love me.

Juliet. I will confess to you that I love him.

Paris. So will you love me. Poor soul, you have been crying again.

Juliet. Are you free now, holy father, or should I come back later?

Friar Laurence. I can help you now, sad daughter. My lord, we must be alone now.

Paris. God forbid I should keep you from prayer. Juliet, early on Thursday I will wake you. Till then, good-bye, and keep this holy kiss.

[*He kisses her cheek and leaves.*]

Juliet. O shut the door, and then come and weep with me, past hope, past cure, past help!

Friar Laurence. Ah Juliet, I know your grief. I am not sure what to do. I hear you must—and nothing can stop it—on this Thursday be married to Count Paris.

Juliet. Don't tell me that you know this unless you tell me how to stop it. If in your wisdom you cannot help, with this knife I'll help myself instantly. God joined my heart and Romeo's. You joined our hands. And before this hand, given by you to Romeo, shall be given to another, this hand shall slay them both. So, give me some advice. You are old and wise. Say it now. I long to die if you have no way to help me.

Friar Laurence. Stop, daughter.[1] I see some hope. It is desperate. If, rather than marry the Count Paris, you have the strength to kill yourself, then you might have the strength to do what

---

[1] Friar Laurence believes that if he doesn't help Juliet, she will kill herself.

I plan. Can you stand being near death to avoid death?

Juliet. Tell me to leap off a cliff, rather than marry Paris; or walk where there are thieves; or go where there are snakes. Chain me with roaring bears, or hide me in a **tomb**[2] covered over with dead men's rattling bones, or tell me to go into a new-made grave, and hide me with a dead man in his **shroud**[3]—things that have made me tremble just to hear about—and I will do it without fear to live the true wife of my sweet love.

Friar Laurence. Stop then. Go home, be merry, say you will marry Paris. Wednesday is tomorrow. Tomorrow night send your nurse out of your room. Take this **vial;**[4] drink what is in it. You will feel cold and sleepy. Your pulse will seem to stop. You will seem to stop breathing. The roses in your lips and cheeks will fade. Your eyes will close. You will look dead for forty-two hours, and then you will wake up as if from a good sleep. When your bridegroom Paris comes in the morning to wake you, you

---

[2] **tomb**—a room or building in which dead bodies are placed, not buried.

[3] **shroud**—a cloth used to cover a dead body.

[4] **vial**—a small bottle.

will appear dead. Then, as we do it here, they will carry you, in your best clothes, uncovered, to the tomb of the Capulets. In the meantime, I will send a letter to Romeo. He will come, and he and I shall be with you when you wake. That very night Romeo will carry you to Mantua, if you are not afraid and can do this.

Juliet. Give it to me. Give it. O do not tell me of fear.

Friar Laurence. [*Giving* Juliet *the vial.*] Go. Be strong and lucky in this. I'll send a friar quickly to Romeo with the message.

Juliet. Love give me strength, and strength shall help me. Farewell, dear father.

[*She exits.*]

ACT FOUR, SCENE TWO

At the Capulets' house, as part of Friar Laurence's plan, Juliet tells her father that she will marry Paris. Capulet decides to move the marriage to the next day, Wednesday.

[*Enter* Capulet, Lady Capulet, Nurse, *and two or three* Servants.]

Capulet. Invite these guests.

[*Exit a* Servant *with the list of guests.*]

Sirrah,[1] go hire twenty good cooks.[2]

[*Another* Servant *leaves.*]

We will not be properly prepared for this celebration. Has my daughter gone to see Friar Laurence?

---

[1] Sirrah—a title used for someone lower than the speaker.
[2] Capulet was going to have a "small" celebration, but he is sending for twenty cooks!

Nurse. Yes, she has.

Capulet. Well, he may help her. She is a spoiled, self-willed child.

[*Enter* Juliet.]

Nurse. Here she comes, and looking very happy.

Capulet. Hello, my headstrong daughter. Where have you been?

Juliet. Where I have learned to repent the sin of not obeying my father. Friar Laurence has told me to beg you to forgive me. [*She kneels.*] Pardon I beg of you. From now on I will do as you say.

Capulet. Send for Count Paris! Tell him of this. I'll have you married tomorrow morning.

Juliet. I met the young lord at Friar Laurence's cell, and told him as much as I modestly could.

Capulet. Why, I am glad. This is well. Stand up. This is as it should be. [*To a* Servant.] Go get the Count. This Reverend Friar Laurence has done well.

Juliet. Nurse, will you help me find what I need for tomorrow?

Lady Capulet. No, we should wait until Thursday. That will be soon enough.

Capulet. Go, Nurse, go with her. We will have this marriage tomorrow.

[*Exit* Juliet *and the* Nurse.]

Lady Capulet. We won't have enough food; it's almost night.

Capulet. Tush, I'll take care of it all. Go help Juliet get ready. I won't go to bed tonight. My heart is very happy since my wayward[3] girl is obedient again.

[*He exits.*]

---

[3] wayward—naughty.

In Juliet's room, Juliet takes the sleeping drug that will make her seem to be dead.

[*Enter* Juliet *and* Nurse.]

Juliet. Yes, this is the best dress. But Nurse, you go and help my mother prepare, for I need to pray for heaven's help. For as you know, I have been sinful.

[*Enter* Lady Capulet.]

Lady Capulet. Are you busy? Do you need my help?

Juliet. No, madam. We have found what we need. Please let me rest. Take Nurse with you. I know you will have your hands full.

Lady Capulet. Good night. Go to bed and rest.

[*Exit* Lady Capulet *and* Nurse.]

Juliet. Farewell. God only knows when we will meet again. I have a cold fear. I'll call them back to comfort me.—Nurse—What could she do here? I must act this sad scene alone. Come, vial. What if this mixture doesn't work? Shall I be married to Paris tomorrow? No! No! [*She picks up a knife.*] This shall stop it. Lie there.

[*She lays down the knife.*]

What if the Friar has given me real poison? What if he doesn't want anyone to know that he married me to Romeo? I fear this is poison. But yet, it cannot be—for he is still a holy man. What if I am laid in the tomb and wake before Romeo comes? Will there be enough air for me to breathe in the tomb? Or, if I live, I will be in a tomb, a place of death and night, where for many years the bones of my buried ancestors have been packed, where Tybalt lies decaying, where there may be ghosts. Alas! If I wake early, I may go mad and play with my ancestor's bones, pull mangled Tybalt from his burial place, and in this madness club my brains out with some old kinsman's bone. O look, I think I see Tybalt's ghost come for Romeo! Stop, Tybalt, stop! Romeo, Romeo, Romeo, here's my drink! I drink to you!

[*She drinks and falls on her bed.*]

At the Capulets' house, the Capulets stay up all night to get ready for the wedding of Juliet to Paris. Paris arrives to marry Juliet.

[*Enter* Lady Capulet *and the* Nurse.]

Lady Capulet. Here, take these keys and get more spices, Nurse.

Nurse. They need dates and apples for the pies.

[*Enter* Capulet.]

Capulet. Come, quickly, quickly, quickly. It's getting late. It's three a.m.

Nurse. Get to bed. You'll be sick tomorrow from lack of sleep.

Capulet. I have stayed up all night for less reason, and not been sick.

Lady Capulet. Yes, and you've been known to chase women, but I will chase you from such chasing now.

[*Exit* Lady Capulet *and* Nurse. *Enter* Servants *with logs.*]

Capulet. Hurry, hurry. You are a log head. The Count will be here soon. Look! It's daylight!

[*Music is heard off stage.*]

I hear him. He is coming! Nurse! Wife! Nurse, I say!

[*Enter* Nurse.]

Go wake up Juliet, get her dressed. I'll go talk with Paris. Hurry. Hurry. The bridegroom is here already. Hurry, I say.

[*Exit* Nurse *and* Capulet *with a* Servant.]

ACT FOUR, SCENE FIVE

In Juliet's room, the Nurse finds Juliet, who looks dead. All are grief-stricken. Friar Laurence and Paris arrive for the wedding, which will now be a funeral.

[*The* Nurse *goes to the curtain hiding the bed.*]

Nurse. Mistress! Juliet! Fast asleep, I guess. Why, lamb, why, lady, shame! You lazy girl! Why, love, I say! Madam! Sweetheart! Bride! Not a word? How sound she sleeps! I have to wake her. Madam, madam, madam! What, dressed already and asleep? I have to wake you. Lady! Lady! Lady! Alas, alas! Help, help! My lady's dead! O terrible day. I wish I had never been born. My lord! My lady!

[*Enter* Lady Capulet.]

Lady Capulet. What is all this noise?

Nurse. O terrible day!

Lady Capulet. What is the matter?

Nurse. Look, look. O heavy day!

Lady Capulet. O me! O me! My child, my only life! Wake up, look at me, or I will die with you. Help, help! Call help!

[*Enter* Capulet.]

Capulet. For shame. Bring Juliet out. Her lord is here.

Nurse. She's dead, dead! She's dead! Alas, the day!

Lady Capulet. Alas the day! She's dead, dead! She's dead!

Capulet. No! Let me see her. Alas. She's cold. Her blood is cold. Life and her lips have long been separated. Death has come like frost and taken the sweetest flower in all the field.

Nurse. O terrible day!

Lady Capulet. O the saddest of all times!

Capulet. Death, that has taken her away to make me cry, ties up my tongue and will not let me speak.

[*Enter* Friar Laurence, Paris, *and* Musicians.]

Friar Laurence. Come, is the bride ready to go to church?

Capulet. Ready to go, but never to return. O son, the night before your wedding day, death has taken your bride. There she lies. Death is my son-in-law. Death has wedded my daughter. I will die, and leave death everything: life, living, all is death's.

Paris. I have waited long to see this morning, and now I see such a terrible sight.

Lady Capulet. Cursed, unhappy, wretched, hateful day! The most miserable hour that time ever saw! I only have one child, one poor and loving child, only one child to have joy in, and cruel death has taken her.

Nurse. O woe![1] O woeful, woeful, woeful day! Most terrible day. Most woeful day that ever I have seen! O hateful day! There never was such a terrible day!

[1] woe—sorrow.

Paris. Tricked, wronged by death. O love! O life! Not life, but love in death!

Capulet. Hated, martyred, killed. Terrible time, why did you come now to murder this wedding? O child, O child! My soul, not just my child. You are dead. Alas, my child is dead, and with my child my joys are buried.

Friar Laurence. Peace, for shame. Confusion will not cure your grief. Heaven and you had a part of this fair maid. Now heaven has all of her. Your part you could not keep from death, but heaven gives her eternal life. You wanted her to be happy. She is happy now. And you weep because she is happy? Dry your tears, put rosemary[2] on this fair corpse, and, as the custom is, carry her to the church in her finest clothes. Our love tells us to cry. But reason tells us to be happy, for she is happy in heaven.

Capulet. Everything we ordered for the wedding shall now be used for the funeral. Our music will be funeral bells. Our wedding feast becomes a funeral feast. Our bridal flowers will be for the corpse. All things change to the opposite.

---

[2] rosemary—a plant used for cooking and medicine. It stands for remembering.

Friar Laurence. Sir, go in, and madam, go with him, and go, Sir Paris. Everyone prepare to follow this body to the grave. Heaven punishes you for some sin.

[*Exit all but the* Nurse, *who closes the curtain on* Juliet.]

*In a different city, Mantua, where Romeo has been living in
exile, Romeo's servant Balthasar brings word that Juliet is
dead. Romeo goes to buy poison to kill himself.*

[*Enter* Romeo.]

Romeo. I have dreamed that some happy news
will come. I have had cheerful thoughts all
day. I dreamed my Juliet came and found me
dead—strange dream—and breathed life into
me with kisses, and I revived and became a
king. Ah me, how sweet is love when even a
dream of love is so rich in joy.

[*Enter* Balthasar, *Romeo's servant. He is dressed in
riding clothes.*]

News from Verona! Balthasar, do you bring me
letters from the Friar? How is my lady? Is my

father well? How is my Juliet? That I can ask again, for nothing can be ill if she be well.

Balthasar. Then she is well, and nothing can be ill. Her body sleeps in the Capulets' tomb, and her immortal soul is with the angels. I saw her laid in her family's tomb and came to tell you. Pardon me for bringing this sad news.

Romeo. Is it so? Then go to my rooms. Get me ink and paper. Hire me horses. I will leave here tonight.

Balthasar. I beg you sir, be patient. You look pale and wild.

Romeo. You are mistaken. Leave me, and do what I told you. Do you have any letters from Friar Laurence?

Balthasar. No, my lord.

Romeo. It doesn't matter. Go. Hire the horses. I'll be with you right away.

[*Exit* Balthasar.]

Well, Juliet, I will lie with you tonight. How shall I do it? O mischief, you are quick to enter into the thoughts of desperate men. I remember an **apothecary**[1]—near here. He looked poor. In his shop hung a stuffed alligator, strange shaped fish, pots, old seeds, and plants. Such a poor man might sell illegal poison. And this same man must sell it to me. This should be his house. Since it is a holiday, the shop is closed. Open up, Apothecary!

Apothecary. Who calls so loudly?

Romeo. Come here, man. I see you need money. Here are forty ducats.[2] Let me have a bottle of poison, something that will work very fast.

Apothecary. Such a poison I have, but the law will not let me sell it. They would kill me if I sold it.

Romeo. Are you so poor and badly off, and still afraid to die? Hunger is in your cheeks, worry is in your eyes, lack of money hangs on your back. The world is not your friend, nor is the world's law. The world doesn't give you a law to get rich. So don't be poor, but break the law, and take this money.

Apothecary. My **poverty**,[3] but not my wish, makes me take this.

---

[1] **apothecary**—person who makes and sells medicine, pharmacist.

[2] ducats—coins.

[3] **poverty**—lack of money.

Romeo. I pay your poverty and not your wish.

Apothecary. Put this in water and drink it. If you had the strength of twenty men, it would kill you right away.

Romeo. Here is your gold—worse poison to men's souls, doing more murder in this world than any poison you might sell. I sell you poison, you have sold me none. Farewell. Buy food and grow fatter. Come medicine,[4] go with me to Juliet's grave. There I will use you.

[*They exit.*]

---

[4] medicine—Romeo calls the poison a medicine.

In Friar Laurence's cell, Friar John tells Friar Laurence why he couldn't deliver the letter telling Romeo about their plan. When he learns this, Friar Laurence goes immediately to the churchyard where Juliet has been placed in the Capulet family tomb.

[*Enter* Friar John.]

Friar John. Holy Friar Laurence, brother. Come out.

Friar Laurence. [*To himself*] This is the voice of Friar John. [*To* Friar John] Welcome from your trip to Mantua. What does Romeo say?

Friar John. When I went to find a brother of our order to travel with me according to our rules, the health officials thought his house was infected. We were shut up.[1] They would not let us out. So I could not take your letter to Romeo.

Friar Laurence. Who took the letter to him?

Friar John. I could not send it—here it is again. They were so afraid of illness that they would not let a messenger bring it to you.

Friar Laurence. Unhappy fortune! This letter was very important. Not sending it may do great harm. Friar John, go find me a crowbar and bring it here quickly.

Friar John. Brother, I'll get it.

[Friar John *exits.*]

Friar Laurence. I must quickly go alone to the tomb of the Capulets. Before three hours are over, Juliet will wake up. She will be angry that Romeo is not there. But I will write to him again and keep Juliet at my cell till Romeo comes. Poor living corpse, closed in a dead man's tomb.

[*He exits.*]

---

[1] Friar John was locked up in a house because the health officials thought the house might have been infected with the bubonic plague, a disease carried by fleas on rats. Plague killed about half the population of Europe in two years.

That night in the churchyard, Romeo and Paris fight. Paris is killed. When Romeo enters the tomb, he sees Juliet, who looks dead. Friar Laurence arrives too late to stop Romeo, who takes the poison. Juliet wakes up. Friar Laurence tries to get Juliet to leave, but she won't. Friar Laurence panics and leaves. Juliet uses Romeo's knife to kill herself. The Prince arrives. Friar Laurence is caught and tells what happened. Too late to save their children, the Capulets and Montagues call a peace and say they will make gold statues of Romeo and Juliet. Peace and order are brought to the city, but too late for Romeo and Juliet.

[*Enter* Paris *and his* Page, *with flowers*]

Paris. Give me the torch, boy. Leave me here alone.
Yet, put out the torch so no one can see me.
Listen, and if you hear anyone coming, whistle
to warn me. Give me the flowers. Do as I say, go.

Page. I am almost afraid to stand alone. Yet I will.

[*He goes off.* Paris *puts the flowers around the tomb.*]

Paris. Sweet flower, with flowers I cover your bridal bed. O sadness, your sheets are dust and stone on which my tears drop. I will bring flowers here every night.

[*The* Page *whistles.*]

The boy warns me of someone coming. What cursed foot comes so late to stop true love's gifts. He carries a torch. Cover me for a while, night.

[Paris *hides.*]

[*Enter* Romeo *and* Balthasar *with a pick and a crowbar.*]

Romeo. Give me that pick and bar. Wait, take this letter. Early in the morning take this to my father. Give me the torch. Promise me that whatever you hear or see, you will not stop me. I go down into this bed of death in part to see my lady's face. But mostly I come to take a ring she wears.[1] So, be gone. If you try to spy on me, I will tear you apart and throw your parts all over this churchyard.

---

[1] Romeo has not come to take a ring that Juliet wears. He is going to kill himself and doesn't want his servant to try to stop him.

Balthasar. I will be gone, sir, and not trouble you.

Romeo. Then you are my friend. Take this. [Romeo *gives* Balthasar *money.*] Live and be well. Good-bye, good fellow.

Balthasar. [*To himself*] For all he says, I'll hide and see if I can help.

[Balthasar *hides.*]

Romeo. You horrible mouth of death[2], filled with the sweetest on this earth. I'll force your rotten jaws open, and stuff you with more food.

[Romeo *pries open the gate to the tomb.*]

Paris. [*To himself*] This is the proud Montague, Romeo, that murdered my love's cousin—which grief I think killed her—and he has come here to do some horrible shame to the dead bodies. I will stop him. [Paris *shouts to* Romeo.] Stop your unholy work, evil Montague. Can you hate the dead? Villain, I have caught you. Obey, and go with me, for you must die.

Romeo. I must indeed. That is why I came here. Good gentle youth, do not tempt a desperate man. Go quickly, and leave here. Think about

---

[2] horrible mouth of death—the tomb.

the dead here. Let them frighten you. I beg you, youth, do not put another sin on my head by making me angry. O, be gone! By heaven, I care more for you than for myself, for I came here armed against myself. Don't stay, be gone. Live, and in the future say a madman's mercy told you to run.

Paris. I arrest you as a criminal.

Romeo. Will you anger me? Then have at you, boy!

[*They fight.*]

Page. O lord, they fight! I will get the guard.

[*Exit* Page.]

Paris. O, I am hurt! If I die and you are merciful, open the tomb, lay me with Juliet.

[Paris *dies.*]

Romeo. In faith, I will. Let me see this face. [Romeo *recognizes* Paris.] Mercutio's kinsman, noble Count Paris! What did my man say when my troubled soul did not listen? I think he said Paris should have married Juliet. Did he say that? Or did I dream it? Or am I mad? O, give me your hand, one written with me in sour misfortune's book. I'll bury you in a triumphant grave. [*He opens the tomb.*]

A grave? No, a great hall lit by Juliet. How often when men are at the point of death do they grow happy? O my love, my wife, death that has sucked the honey of your breath has no power yet over your beauty. You are not conquered. Beauty's flag is still on your lips and in your cheeks. And death's pale flag is not there yet.[3]

Tybalt, do you lie there in your bloody sheet? O, what more favor can I do you than with the hand that killed your youth to kill he who was your enemy? Forgive me, cousin.

Ah, dear Juliet, why are you still so beautiful? Shall I believe that death loves you too? For fear of that I will stay with you, and never leave this palace of darkness again. Here, here will I stay with worms that are your maids. O, here will be my everlasting rest. Eyes, look your last. Arms, take your last embrace! And lips, O you doors

---

[3] Romeo says that death has no power over Juliet: she doesn't look dead. Of course, she isn't dead, but he doesn't know it. This is *dramatic irony*: the audience knows something that contradicts what the characters say.

of breath, seal with a kiss an everlasting bargain with death. [*He kisses* Juliet.] Come, bitter guide, pilot this seasick weary ship onto the rocks. Here's to my love!

[*He drinks the poison.*]

O true Apothecary, your drugs are quick. Thus with a kiss I die.

[*Enter* Friar Laurence *with a lantern, crowbar, and shovel.*]

Friar Laurence. Saint Francis help me. How often tonight have my old feet stumbled on graves. Who's there?

Balthasar. I'm a friend who knows you well.

Friar Laurence. Bless you. Tell me, good friend, whose light is that which burns here? It burns on the Capulets' tomb.

Balthasar. It does, sir, and there you will find my master, someone you love.

Friar Laurence. Who is it?

Balthasar. Romeo.

Friar Laurence. How long has he been there?

Balthasar. A full half hour.

Friar Laurence. Go with me to the tomb.

Balthasar. I dare not, sir. My master thinks I have left. He threatened me with death if I stayed.

Friar Laurence. Stay then. I'll go alone. I am afraid. O, much I fear what might have happened.

Balthasar. As I slept here under this yew tree, I dreamed my master and another man fought, and my master killed him.

Friar Laurence. Romeo!

[*The* Friar *sees the blood and weapons.*]

Alas, alas, what blood stains the stony entrance of this tomb? Why are these bloody swords lying by this place of peace? Romeo! O so pale! Who else? What, Paris too? And covered with blood? What an unkind hour.—The lady wakes up.

[Juliet *wakes.*]

Juliet. O comforting Friar, where is my lord? I do remember where I should be, and there I am. Where is my Romeo?

Friar Laurence. I hear a noise. Lady, come out of this nest of death, disease, and unnatural sleep. A greater power has ruined our plan. Come, come away. Your husband next to you lies dead. And Paris too. Come, I'll take you to a **convent**.[4] Don't stop to ask questions. The guard is coming. Come, good Juliet. I dare not stay any longer.

Juliet. Go, get away, for I will not leave.

[*Exit* Friar Laurence.]

What's here? A cup in my true love's hand? Poison, I see, has caused his death. O rude man, you have drunk all of it and left no friendly drop to help me follow you. I will kiss your lips. Perhaps some poison still hangs on them to make me die.

[*She kisses him.*]

Your lips are warm!

Watchman. [*Off stage*] Show me, boy. Which way?

Juliet. A noise? Then I'll be quick. O happy dagger. This is your **sheath**.[5] There rest, and let me die.

[*She stabs herself and falls on* Romeo's *body. Enter* Page *and* Watchmen.]

Page. This is the place. There, where the torch burns.

---

[4] **convent**—a house where nuns live. Nuns leave everyday life and enter a life of service and prayer. Friar Laurence believes that so much has happened that Juliet cannot return to her former life.

[5] **sheath**—a case for a sword or dagger when it is not being used.

1st Watchman. The ground is bloody. Search around the churchyard. Go, some of you. Whoever you find, arrest.

[*They search.*]

2nd Watchman. Here's Romeo's man. We found him in the churchyard.

1st Watchman. Hold him until the Prince gets here.

[*Enter another* Watchman *with* Friar Laurence.]

3rd Watchman. Here is a Friar that trembles, sighs, and weeps. We took this shovel and pick from him as he was leaving the churchyard.

1st Watchman. Very **suspicious.**[6] Keep the Friar too.

[*Enter the* Prince *and* Attendants.]

Prince. What evil has called us from our morning rest?

[*Enter* Capulet *and* Lady Capulet.]

Capulet. What is happening?

Lady Capulet. O, some people in the street are crying "Romeo," some "Juliet," and some "Paris." And all run toward this tomb.

---

[6] **suspicious**—something that makes one suspect, doubtful.

Prince. What fear is this which startles us now?

1st Watchman. Prince, here lies the Count Paris dead, and Romeo dead, and Juliet, dead before, warm, and newly killed.

Prince. Search, seek. Let us find how this evil murder happened.

1st Watchman. Here is a Friar, and dead Romeo's man, with tools to open these tombs.

Capulet. O heavens! O wife, look how our daughter bleeds! This dagger is mistaken. It belongs to Montague and is sheathed in our daughter's bosom.[7]

Lady Capulet. O me! This sight of death is a bell that tells me of my own death.

[*Enter* Montague *and* Servants.]

Prince. Come, Montague, you are up early to see your son down early.

Montague. Alas, my lord, my wife died tonight. Sorrow for my son's exile killed her. What more sorrow can happen to this old man?

Prince. Look, and you will see.

---

[7] bosom—breast.

Montague. O, I did not teach you right, Romeo! What bad manners it is to go to your grave before your father.

Prince. Control your sorrow until we can find what really happened here. Then I will lead you in sorrow. Meantime, bring to me the parties who helped in this.

Friar Laurence. I am the most involved in this murder and was able to do least. I stand here to accuse and excuse myself.

Prince. Then quickly say what you know about these deaths.

Friar Laurence. I will be brief.[8] Romeo, there dead, was husband to Juliet; and she, there dead, was Romeo's faithful wife. I married them, and their secret marriage day was the day Tybalt died. Tybalt's death sent Romeo away, and Juliet cried for Romeo, not for Tybalt. You, her father, to remove her grief, would have had her marry Paris. She came to me for a plan to stop the marriage, or she would have killed herself then. I gave her a drink to make her sleep. It made her look dead. Meantime I wrote

---

[8] Now comes a long explanation of what we already know. Modern audiences probably don't like it. Maybe Shakespeare's audience didn't either. It does help make clear all the fast action at the end of the play.

to Romeo explaining all and asking him to be here when she woke. My letter did not get to him. I came here all alone to take her where she could wait until Romeo could come for her. But I came too late. Here lay the noble Paris and the faithful Romeo. She woke. I begged her to leave with me. A noise scared me from the tomb, but she would not go with me. It seems she killed herself. All this I know. Her Nurse knew about the marriage. If this is my fault, let the law end my old life.

Prince. I have known you as a holy man. Where's Romeo's man? What can he add to the story?

Balthasar. I brought my master news of Juliet's death. He quickly came here. He told me to give this letter to his father and would kill me if I followed him into the tomb.

Prince. Give me the letter. I will read it. Where is Count Paris's page that called the guards? Sirrah, what was the Count Paris doing here?

Page. He came with flowers for his lady's grave, and sent me away, so I went away. Soon someone came with a light and tools to open the tomb. He and my master fought, and I ran away to call the guards.

Prince. This letter proves the Friar's story is true. It tells of their love, her supposed death, the buying of poison, and Romeo coming to this tomb to die beside her. Where are these enemies? Capulet, Montague, see what pain is caused by your hate. Heaven finds a way to kill your joys with love. And I, too, for not stopping you, have lost kinsmen. We are all punished.

Capulet. O brother Montague, give me your hand. This is all the gift I wish from you in exchange for my daughter in marriage.

Montague. But I will give you more. I will have a golden statue of her made. While this city lasts, there shall never be a statue so valuable as that of true and faithful Juliet.

Capulet. Romeo's statue shall be as rich. This is a very little to give for our hate.

Prince. A gloomy peace is made this morning. The sun, for sorrow, is hiding and will not shine. Let us go talk more of these sad things. Some shall be pardoned, and some punished, for never was a story of more sadness told than this of Juliet and her Romeo.

[*They exit.*]